G000155914

MADEIRA and PORTO SANTO

WINDRUSH · ISLAND GUIDES

MADEIRA and PORTO SANTO

Andrew Gravette

THE WINDRUSH PRESS
GLOUCESTERSHIRE

Acknowledgements

The Author's grateful thanks go to The Portuguese National Tourist Office, London, UK and The Secretaria Regional do Tourismo e Cultura, Funchal, Madeira for their kind assistance in compiling this book. Thanks are also due to 3M Scotch Film.

First published in Great Britain by
The Windrush Press,
Windrush House,
Main Street,
Adlestrop, Moreton-in-Marsh,
Gloucestershire
1990

British Library Cataloguing in Publication Data
Gravette, A. Gerald, (Andrew Gerald)
    Madeira and Porto Santo – (Windrush island guide).
    1. Portugal. Madeira – Visitors' guides
    I. Title
    914.69'80444

    ISBN 0-900075-51-1

Typeset by DP Photosetting, Aylesbury, Bucks
Printed and bound in Great Britain by
The Bath Press, Avon

CONTENTS

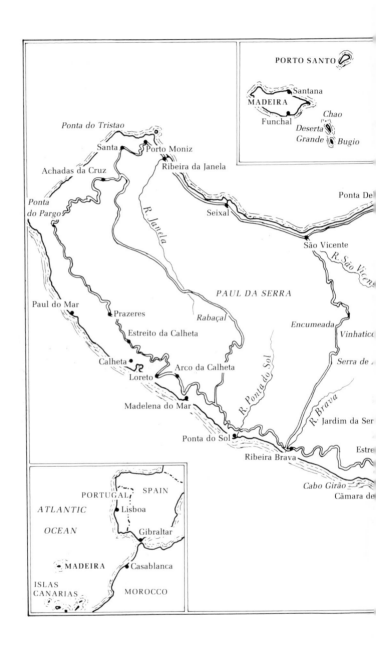

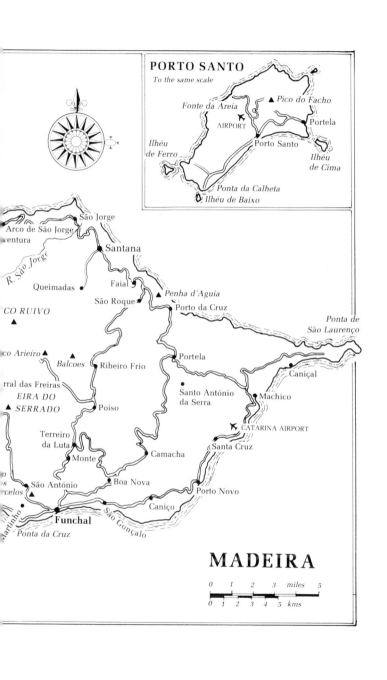

PORTO SANTO
To the same scale

Fonte da Areia
▲ Pico do Facho
AIRPORT
Portela
Ilhéu
de Ferro
Porto Santo
Ilhéu
de Cima
Ponta da Calheta
Ilhéu de Baixo

São Jorge
Arco de São Jorge
ventura
R. São Jorge
Santana
Queimadas
Faial
Penha d'Aguia
São Roque
Porto da Cruz
CO RUIVO
▲
Ponta de
São Laurenço
co Arieiro ▲
▲
Balcoes
Ribeiro Frio
Portela
Caniçal
rral das Freiras
Santo António
da Serra
Machico
EIRA DO
SERRADO
Poiso
CATARINA AIRPORT
Terreiro
da Luta
Santa Cruz
Monte
Camacha
o
s
celos
São António
Boa Nova
Porto Novo
Caniço
Martinho
Funchal
São Gonçalo
Ponta da Cruz

MADEIRA

0   1   2   3   miles   5
0 1 2 3 4 5 kms

INTRODUCTION

Take vines from the Mediterranean, the rose bush from England, palms from Africa, hibiscus from the isles of the tropics and the giant hardwoods of the Americas; carpet a tiny clutch of mountains and valleys with ferns, heathers, cactus and shrubs from the four corners of the earth; liberally sprinkle rich, volcanic soil over the plot and plant with every imaginable fruit tree and vegetable plant; float the entire cornucopia out to an anchorage in the middle of an ocean, brush with warm, southerly breezes and top with a puff-ball of cloud – and you have the basic ingredients of the island of Madeira.

The sister islands of Porto Santo, Ilhas Desertas and Ilhas Selvagens add long, sandy beaches, rocky desert shores and wild, barren islets to the group that is the archipelago of Madeira. However, without including the 300,000 friendly islanders who welcome visitors to share their moderate climate, bountiful produce and stunning landscape, this island creation would only be a floating wilderness devoid of the essential human hands needed to tend this Atlantic Eden. Over a period of almost 600 years tenacious Madeirans have tamed the wild, ruggedly beautiful countryside and carved an enviably peaceful way of life from their isolated island.

Dubbed the 'Floating Garden', 'Enchanted Isle' and 'Ocean Paradise', Madeira offers a restful retreat from the hectic pace of twentieth-century living. Life on the island is conducted at a leisurely pace and Madeirans unhurriedly go about tending their terraced vines, plots of fruit trees and vegetables, or reaping the bounty of the seas in their gaily-painted fishing boats. Everyday life on Madeira has changed little since Portuguese settlers first cleared the great forests from this 'Isle of Wood'. Today it is not the fifteenth-century explorer, seeking new lands to claim; the sixteenth-century pioneer, carving his farm from the overgrown island; the seventeenth-century pirate, plundering the island's towns and villages; the eighteenth-century sugar and wine barons building luxurious estates; nor is it the Victorian colonials retreating from the tropics to a life of

View of Porto Cruz on Madeira's north coast

peaceful retirement who arrive on the shores of this fascinating island – it is the discerning traveller and the discriminating tourist who share, if only for a short while, the natural riches of Madeira with the hospitable islanders.

Madeira and its delights is an island not to be rushed. It is not a brash resort or a hive of high-life activity. The pace on Madeira is sedate and visitors take time to savour the island's natural luxuries. Madeira, like its famed Malmsey wine, should be sipped, only then can its secrets be properly appreciated. The ever-present scent of exotic blooms carried on stiff sea breezes mingles with the aroma of homely Madeiran cooking and perfume of the island's famous wine. Rising from the Atlantic Ocean waters, black craggy cliffs, striated with emerald terraces, edge a crumpled terrain of lush valleys and sharp volcanic peaks – a backdrop to tranquillity and a very special island that is unforgettable.

GETTING THERE

For many centuries the port of Funchal provided shelter for international shipping, with boats plying routes between Europe and the continents of America, Africa and Asia. Britain established traditional links through trade with Madeira over a period of three hundred years and, for this reason, the island became a favourite of travellers during colonial times. Madeira was an accepted acclimatisation stop-over for military and business personnel returning from long stints in Africa or India. The moderate climate and relaxed atmosphere of Madeira offered a midway haven from the tropics before embarking on the final leg of the voyage to Portugal, France or England. After the days of trading schooners and passenger barques putting into Funchal from long ocean trips, steamships and cruise liners brought visitors to Madeira establishing it as a holiday destination. From 1949 to 1959 Aquila Airways provided a sea-plane service from Southampton to the island, via Lisbon.

The popularity of the island grew with European tourists and Madeira became a fashionable, sub-tropical resort. A number of wealthy families moved to Madeira permanently from Europe – especially from England. The fresh, oceanic air, healthy food and moderate, reliable climate attracted visitors who were recuperating from illnesses and the elderly in their retirement. Today this idyllic destination is becoming increasingly popular as a retreat from the hubbub of modern living and tourists flock to the island, now so much closer to Europe because of improved transport links.

BY AIR

Madeira is about three-and-a-half hours on a direct flight from London and about five-and-a-half hours from both New York and Montreal. As Madeira is Portuguese, the national airline, TAP-Air Portugal, provides a service to both the main island of Madeira and to Porto Santo. Flights from Lisbon, Portugal's capital, arrive daily and there are regular TAP flights from the UK and USA (via Lisbon).

Santa Caterina, Madeira's international airport

Other airlines which fly directly to Madeira from the UK include Air Europe and GB Airways. Many charter aircraft also fly into Santa Catarina, the island's main airport and package tours utilising charter flights are a favourite and economical way of visiting Madeira. Flight only prices from the UK range from about £140–£210.

Madeira is one-and-a-half hours by air from Lisbon. Porto Santo is twenty minutes by air from Santa Catarina airport and there are daily connections – the price is around £25. Madeira's modern airport is just 14 miles (22 kms.) from the island's capital, Funchal, and taxis or public buses make the transfer. There are no porters at the airport.
TAP-Air Portugal is on Avenida do Mar, Funchal. Tel: 23061.

BY SEA

Madeira is an internationally popular stop-over for cruise liners and the large port of Funchal, with its long Molhe da Pontinha, or harbour arm, always has one or two cruise ships moored alongside its quay. Most major passenger shipping lines and numerous smaller lines include Madeira in their sailing itineraries. Popular times of the year for cruising to Madeira are Christmas and New Year when there are portside festivities to enjoy. For sailing boat visitors the large Marina at Funchal, near the City Dock, is fully equipped and has berths for up to 120 craft. Call sign (VHF) channel 16: 'Marina'; working channel on 11-1-28/

60-88. Tel: 22545. Also contact Amigos do Mar, Rota do Atlantico, Funchal, for boat excursions and the city's Naval Club.

The Porto Santo ferry, an often bumpy trip on the *Indepencia* hydrofoil, takes about one-and-a-half hours, and makes daily excursions (twice a day in summer) from Funchal's centrally located quay to Porto Santo (Vila Baleira). The cost is around £10. Other, less regular, ferries make trips from the same wharf to Ponta de São Lourenço, Madeira's easternmost port, Ponto do Sol on the island's south coast, and the Ilhas Desertas, 11 miles (18 kms.) to the south-east.

VISITOR'S HINTS

British, American and Canadian passport holders need no visa to enter this autonomous region of Portugal, which is within the EEC. Stays can be made for up to 60 days without a visa and this period can be extended upon application to the authorities.

Contact: Portuguese Consulate General, 62 Brompton Road. London SW3. Telephone (01) 581 8722.

Portuguese National Tourist Office, New Bond Street House, 1/5 New Bond Street London, W1Y 0NP. Telephone (01) 493 3873.

Portuguese National Tourist Office, 548 Fifth Avenue, New York, NY 10036-5089. Telephone (212) 354 4403-7.

Portuguese National Tourist Office, 1801 McGill College Ave. Suite 1020, Montreal. Telephone 514 282 1264.

Permits can be applied for at the above addresses for either residency or employment in Madeira and these should be obtained, if required, before entering the island. Currency, health and customs regulations should all be checked before travelling to Madeira.

TRAVEL ON MADEIRA

Early visitors to Madeira, particularly those on a day's sightseeing stop-over, either outwardbound for the topics, or on the home run to Europe, would make the most of their time on the island by taking advantage of the various old-fashioned forms of transport. Sailing ships anchored off Funchal and small launches would ferry passengers into the port. The Molhe da Pontinha quay, begun at the end of the eighteenth century, was not completed until 1962.

The gentry were then transported by ox-cart, to Monte and Terreiro da Luta, high above the island's capital. These carts, known as *Carros de Bois*, were actually carriages on wooden runners instead of conventional wheels. The cart's runners slid with ease over the steep, cobbled slopes and gave visitors a comfortable ride. This unusual form of transport was designed by a Captain Bulkeley of the English Life Guards when he was stationed on the hilly island and initially had one made for himself and one for his wife. Prior to the invention of the ox-cart, two men, with a *hamac*, or hammock, slung between them, would carry travellers up the hill roads to see Funchal's famous sights.

After taking the mountain air and visiting the surround-

The traditional *Carros de Bois* sledge

ing peaks and beauty spots, visitors would then climb into wickerwork toboggans for the exciting return trip down smooth cobbled streets to the portside a couple of thousand feet below. These toboggans were also an innovation of the English. A Mr Gordon, who lived high above Madeira's capital, used to amuse himself by hurtling down the steep road into Funchal on a sled. Later, this form of vehicle, known locally as the *Carros de Cesto*, was adapted to take two people and steered and controlled by two operators using ropes to restrain the craft on its downward flight. These drivers in traditional garb, who ran alongside the basket-work carriages, had their craft transported back up to Monte, in the hills above the city, by lorries and took a taxi ride up themselves to wait for their next passengers. From the late 1900s until 1943, the trip from Funchal into the mountains could be made by funicular railway, a service now discontinued.

Today one can still experience the ox-cart rides in Funchal and sled runs from Monte to the harbour. However, for the longer-term visitor there is no better way of seeing Madeira and its towns and villages, than by taking a walking tour from designated points on the island. The best way of getting to any selected walk is by hiring a car. There are also taxis and local buses which traverse the island. Bicycles can be rented on the flatter island of Porto Santo but there is no provision for car hire on this smaller island.

Roads are winding and steep on Madeira and care should be taken, not only of other traffic, but also of animals and children straying onto the roads. Speeds should be kept to a minimum. Be warned, in the countryside there are few petrol stations and garages are only located in large towns. Garage Ivens and Garage Nunes, both on Rua Ivens, Funchal, are contactable on Tels: 23 872 and 20 542 respectively. A good road hugs the often steep-cliffed coast of Madeira island, four main routes cross the island from north to south and several smaller roads run up to sightseeing locations, beauty spots and mountain peaks. Several roads are inaccessible to motor vehicles and the driver should take heed of road signs. On Porto Santo a main road runs along the south coast and several minor roads reach into the interior of the island. Only one small road crosses Porto Santo from north to south.

The Madeira Tourist Office in Funchal stocks several

brochures with road maps of the islands and there are bookshops which sell detailed maps that are useful when driving independently. A small phrase book can also be handy for the motorist.

CAR HIRE

National and international self-drive car hire companies operate on Madeira and there is a chauffeur service available. A valid foreign licence is needed and the minimum age for hiring a car on the islands is 23. Renaults, Fiestas, Escorts, Opels, Marbellas and Mini Mokes are the usual vehicles available. Cars can be rented at Santa Catarina airport or can be organised from most hotels – although there may be a delivery and pick-up charge. Telephone numbers for some of the car hire firms are: Atlas – Shell Station, Infante, 23 100/29 672; Avis – Largo Antonio, 64 546/63 495; Hertz 26 026/23 332; Ivens, 23 872.

Car Hire Examples (approximate)

£ Sterling:	3 Days	7 Days	Daily Add-on
Renault 5	69	140	23
Mini Moke	69	166	25
Ford Fiesta	83	185	28
Ford Escort	99	227	35

A day's hire of a Marbella is around £20; of a Fiesta, about £26, and a Renault 11 for a day will cost around £30.

PETROL

The price of petrol on Madeira generally works out a little more expensive that the cost in Britain, around £2.10 per gallon, 46p per litre.

TAXIS

There are a number of taxi firms on Madeira which can be contacted from the airport or most hotels, and fares are not excessive for moderate journeys. Some taxis on the island are picturesque vintage and veteran vehicles.

However, the most photogenic mode of transport must be the ox-sled. In Funchal, pairs of oxen draw covered, wickerwork sledges called *Carros de Bois* along the smooth cobbled streets – a slow, but thoroughly enjoyable way of seeing the sights and city life at close quarters. Similar, but more of an entertainment, are the gravity-powered toboggans known as *Carros de Cesto*, which are propelled down steep cobbled slopes by boater-wearing operators. These twin-seater wicker sleds hurtle the tourists on sleigh rides from the hillside villages of Monte or Terriro da Luta, to Funchal on the coast.

BUS SERVICES

An excellent local bus service offers the traveller an easy and economical method of getting around the island. Bus stops are signposted 'Paragem' and the Tourist Office in Funchal can provide timetables and route maps. The bus routes operate almost all over the island and are run by a number of private enterprises.

Telephone numbers for two of the coach tour companies are: Agência Abreu, Rua Gorgulho, Tel: 31 077 and Panorama Viagens e Turismo, Rua Dr Brito Camara. Tel: 29 194.

LINKS TO PORTO SANTO

The approximate cost of a flight from Santa Catarina airport on Madeira to Porto Santo is around £25 and the price of the journey by sea, either by ferry or hydrofoil, is about £10. The flight is much preferred to the sea voyage as it is not only much shorter but much more comfortable than the sea crossing and is not reliant on weather conditions.

TAXI AND BUS LINKS

From Santa Catarina airport to the capital, Funchal, costs about £3 by taxi and around £1 by bus but most tour companies arrange for coach transfers from the airport to hotel and back.

OTHER TRANSPORT

From Funchal and some of Madeira's larger ports, it is possible to join motor launch excursions around the island giving passengers a new and unusual angle from which to view the spectacular coastal scenery. It is also planned to run a series of helicopter trips around the island for visitors to enjoy Madeira's remarkable terrain from the air.

HOTELS AND RESTAURANTS

The hotels on Madeira rate from one to five stars, and they range from luxury-style hotels to apartment hotels, motels, pensions, or pensãos, inns and self-catering establishments. There are a total of 70 listed tourist accommodations on Madeira, more than 50 of which are situated in or around Funchal. Two large hotels are located either side of the capital. In Machico there are three hotels and in Canico just two. Portuguese government-run hotels situated in beauty spots or locations of historic interest are known as Pousadas. There are only two Pousadas on Madeira, situated in the centre of the island. On Porto Santo there are three listed hotels and two pensions.

FUNCHAL

Most Funchal hotels are around 30 minutes drive from Santa Catarina airport and, although they all deserve a mention, some warrant a short description.

REIDS * * * * *

Probably the most famous hotel on the island of Madeira is Reids. This 100-year-old, 168 bedroom establishment was founded by a William Reid from Scotland and it stands in ten acres of mature sub-tropical garden. Ideally positioned on a headland to the west of Funchal with fantastic views, this elegant Madeiran institute has two heated sea water pools, health centre and sauna and sports facilities including tennis, billiards and all manner of watersports available from its little cove.
Tel: 23 001.

CASINO PARK * * * * *

This luxury hotel's 400 rooms include 20 suites and 32 junior suites all with private balconies and stunning views. The island's only casino and conference centre are part of this clifftop complex which is a few minutes' walk from the

The architect of Brasilia designed the Casino Park Hotel

capital's town centre. Pool, tennis, gymnasium, sauna and nightclub are just a few of the facilities offered in this deluxe hotel which was devised by the architect responsible for designing Brasilia, Oscar Niemeyer.
Tel: 33 111.

SAVOY * * * * *

Overlooking Funchal Bay, this charming top-class hotel has 341 rooms. Four pools, two tennis courts, mini-golf and nightly dancing are some of the attractions here, not to mention the glorious sea views. Conference and banquet facilities are provided and the entire complex is set in luxurious gardens high above the capital. In a traditional house set in the gardens are the Apartments Royale.
Tel: 22 031.

MADEIRA PALACIO * * * * *

With a backdrop of the world's second highest cliff, the views from this 260-room, 18-suite hotel are stupendous. One of the leading hotels on the island, and set in magnificent gardens, the facilities here include two tennis courts and one badminton court plus heated pool and conference rooms.
Tel: 30 001.

MADEIRA SHERATON * * * * *

Set on a cliffside just a ten minute walk from the city centre, this stylish hotel, with 292 bedrooms and 15 suites, has three pools, tennis, mini-golf and a health club. Grill, taverna, bar, English pub, seventeenth-century style restaurant and magnificent Funchal Bay views are just a few of the facilities offered in this luxurious establishment. An extension of the hotel is the Madeira Beach Club apartments located on the sea front.
Tel: 72 122.

GIRASSOL * * * *

This is one of the leading four-star hotels in Funchal and accommodation here includes balconies in the 136 rooms, heated pool and lido complex. Two bars, TV lounge, international restaurant and panoramic views complete the range of facilities of this friendly hotel.
Tel: 29 281

OUTSIDE FUNCHAL

Other luxury four-star hotels, aparthotels and guesthouses surrounding Funchal include the Quinta do Sol, 118 rooms, 7 suites; Hotel Raga, 159 rooms; Vila Ramos, 108 rooms; São João, 208 rooms; Alto Lido, 115 rooms; Santa Isabel 68 rooms, 10 suites; Catedral, 25 rooms; Do Mar, 135 rooms; Penha da França, 35 rooms; Navio Azul, 42 rooms, 4 suites; Vila Camacho, Madeira Regency Club, Eden Mar and Vila Vincencia.

CITY CENTRE

Examples of two typical, moderately expensive three-star city centre hotels might be the Windsor, located in the heart of Funchal near the shopping centre with 67 rooms in a modern building with small roof-top pool, snack bar, lounge; or the Monte Carlo with its classically imposing frontage in an old quarter of Funchal with 45 rooms, terrace pool, lounge, bar and shows featuring 'Fado' music and traditional dancing.

Other hotels and guesthouses in Funchal include Hotel do Carmo, 80 rooms; Estrelícia, 148 rooms; Orquídea, 70 rooms and Santa Maria, 83 rooms.

APARTMENTS

These include Aparthotel America, 110 apartments; Apartamento do Mar, 136 rooms; Apartamento Buganvilea, 106 rooms; Golden Gate, 35 rooms; Torre, 41 rooms; Santa Lucia, 22 rooms; Reno, 37 rooms; Casa Branca, 37 rooms, Duas Torres, 118 rooms; Florassol, 89 rooms; Gorgulho, 115 rooms; Lido-Sol, 39 rooms; Mimosa, 100 rooms; Albergaria.

PENSIONS

Pension/residential hotels are popular and include the Astoria, 16 rooms; Greco, 28 rooms; Monaco, 12 rooms, Parque, 22 rooms; Phelps, 18 rooms; Monte Rosa, 39 rooms; Monumental, 24 rooms; Flamenga, 35 rooms; Avenida, 12 rooms; Santa Clara, 14 rooms; Funchal, 12 rooms; Colombo, 25 rooms; Madeira, 31 rooms, 6 suites.

POUSADAS

Pousada do Arieiro compares with a four-star hotel and is located high up in the Pico do Arieiro mountain north of Funchal. Ideal for hikers, this pousada has 18 rooms, restaurant, lounge and bar.

Pousada dos Vinháticos is located north-west of Funchal on the route to Encumeada, and has 11 beautifully kept rooms with restaurant, lounge and bar.

MACHICO

The four hotels in this town near the airport in the south-east of Madeira include the luxurious Hotel Atlantis with 300 rooms and 25 suites. Magnificently situated on the Baía de Zarco, this hotel has a wealth of facilities with tennis, badminton, pool and sauna. Also with pool, tennis and conference facilities, the Hotel Dom Pedro Baía, 218 rooms, is located on the bay not far from the island's Santo da Serra golf course. Dom Pedro Machico also specialises in deep-sea game fishing and water sports. Aldeamento Turistico Matur, near to Machico, is a holiday club and has 272 rooms in various combinations of apartments. This establishment boasts an Olympic-size swimming pool, international bridge club and fine tennis facilities. The Salomar, also in Machico, with 44 rooms, is a residential hotel.

CANIÇO AND GARAJAU

In Caniço there is a large holiday village on Ponta dos Reis Magos called Aldeamento Reis Magos and another on Ponta de Garajua, the Aldeamento Atlas. Between them these two complexes total about 5,000 rooms. They are located to the east of Funchal. On the Garajau side, the Hotel Dom Pedro Garajau has three swimming pools, tennis, and various entertainments. Located between Garajau and Caniço the Aparthotel Inter-Atlas has 133 rooms and swimming pool among other attractions. At Caniço itself there is the Pensão-Residencial Galomar with 36 rooms and sports facilities. On the cliffside south coast is the modernistic Hotel Roca Mar with three bars, pool and diving club.

SANTA CRUZ

In Santa Cruz, between Machico and the capital, the Pensão Matos has 10 rooms and, up in the mountains above Machico, the Santo de Serra, in the health resort town of the same name, has accommodation for around 50 guests. On the north side of the island, in the town of Santana, Pensão Figueira has more than a dozen rooms and, on the north-western tip of Madeira, at Porto Moniz, there are two 20-roomed guesthouses, the Lar de Baía and the Pensão Fernandes. In one of the main towns of the south-west, Calheta, the Porto Santo hotel has 210 rooms.

RESTAURANTS

IN AND AROUND FUNCHAL

Apart from the excellent fare to be enjoyed in the comfort of a hotel, there is a lot of enjoyment in eating in Madeira's local cafés, snack bars, bar-restaurants and top grill rooms. On Madeira, eating places are categorised into four classes from the luxurious to the plain homely. In Funchal there are a bewildering number of good restaurants of which several are recommended here.

For fish dishes, delicacies in which the Madeiran island-ers excel, try the Golfinho Restaurant on Largo do Corpo Santo, just off the corniche, Estrela do Mar, almost next door, or the Gavinas, to the west of Funchal, near the Lido. In the old part of the city, the Romana serves first-class

A bonus of the island's climate is being able to eat outside

meat and fish dishes and, for local specialities try the O
Arco, or the Apolo in the heart of the town. Italian dishes
can be savoured at Clube de Turismo on Estrada Monumental, overlooking the sea and, further into town is the
Casa Velha, near the Pontina quay, which serves international cuisine. Austrian specialities are served at the
Taverna Real and the Chanceler, near the Post Office,
provides international food but includes a variety of regional
dishes on its menu. Try the Café Belin or the centrally
located Cervejaria Coral for local and imported beers. For
exotic dining locations try the yacht *Vagrant*, once owned by
the Beatles, now a luxury restaurant. Alternatively why not
eat freshly caught fish in a seaside cave on Pria Formosa,
Estarda Monumental, or at A Gruta's, built into fortified
battlements. The Kon-Tiki has a glass-covered terrace
where diners can enjoy the excellent international cuisine.

Other restaurants, snack bars, cafés and bars in and near
Funchal include the Caravela, the Charola, A Flor, the
Carochinha and the Patio all in the centre of Funchal. The
São Pedro is near the town centre, the Minas Gerais is out
on Avenida Arriaga and the A Seta and A Brisa are located
up towards Monte to the north of Funchal city centre. Don't
forget Joe's Bar for daytime snacks and evening activity.

MONTE

Just north of Funchal, in the town of Monte, where the
famous sledge rides start from, the Café do Parque is a well-
known eating place for snacks.

CAMANCHA

In Camancha, to the north-east of the capital, Café Relogio specialises in good local fare and the wickerwork shop, José Nobrega, has a restaurant and bar. On the coast road, the Girassol, Jardim Sol, Boieiro and A Lareira bar-restaurants all offer Madeiran specialities.

PORTO MONIZ

Across the island, one of the island's most original restaurants for both regional cuisine and breathtaking scenery, the Cachalote, is set into the cliffside at Porto Moniz. Nearby one might also try the restaurant at the Pensão Fernandez for local dishes, or the Lar de Baia.

SÃO VINCENTE

Also on the north coast, clustered around the small town of São Vincente, there is a choice of five good restaurants including the Quebra Mar in its idyllic coastline setting and the Galeao.

FAIAL

Just around the coast, at Faial, near the popular tourist spot of Santana one can get an excellent meal in stunning surroundings at the Casa de Chia.

SANTO DE SERRA

A little further along, at Santo de Serra, the island's only golf course has a restaurant.

MACHICO

Nearer to Funchal, there are five more little restaurants to choose from in the region of Machico, try O Facho for its succulent seafood, or Mercado Velho for quick snacks.

MATUR

In the Commercial Centre at Matur, near Santa Catarina airport, there is the choice of either Italian cooking at Luigi's or excellent Madeiran cuisine at the Vilao restaurant.

CANIÇO

At Caniço try the O Boeiro for local food, or the Jardim do Sol.

CÂMARA DE LOBOS

The other side of Funchal, at the beauty spot of Câmara de Lobos cliff site are the Ribamar, the Capoeira and a Coral Beer Bar.

CALHETA

Much further along the south coast, at Calheta, the Estrela, or 'Star of Calheta', offers tempting traditional fare.

There are numerous small restaurants across the island, either set on the rocky coastline with spectacular marine views, or located high in the mountain ranges with steep terraces and levada scenes. Not only does the island offer fantastic scenery to complement the wide selection of foods produced on Madeira, but the climate smiles kindly on those who prefer verandah meals or outdoor picnics. It is one of the delights of a Madeiran visit to explore the island and suddenly come across one of the island's 40-or-so country restaurants.

The picturesque fishing village of Câmara de Lobos

ENTERTAINMENT

Most hotels put on a variety of entertainments from 'Fado' music and local dancing demonstrations to full-blown floor shows and, of course there is always the distraction of Madeira's one casino at Casino Park. Many hotels also have their own nightclubs but there is a good deal of nightlife in the city itself. Try Bar Marcelino off Rua Bela de S. Teago, near the east end of the esplanade, specialising in traditional 'Fado' music. Canape Club is nearby as is Casa Portugesa whilst Heaven & Hell is right in the city centre. Further out west are the Prince Albert, a club with a Victorian-style atmosphere to match and Joe's Bar.

For the more sedate, the many halls in the city offer selections of either theatrical productions, orchestral concerts and even ballet performances. Local festivals provide a colourful distraction in outlying villages and the firework display in Funchal at the celebration of the feast of St Sylvester on 31 December is a particularly spectacular event.

PORTO SANTO

HOTELS

There are just five hotels on this small island and the Porto Santo is the largest with 90 rooms, tennis, pool, entertainments and all manner of watersports. Bicycles are available here for touring the island.
Tel: 98 2381/5.

Vila Adelaide is a rustic, traditional-style small villa suitable for family self-catering. Hotel Praia Dourada has 35 rooms, Pensão Palmeira (Tel: 982112) has 23 and Pensão Central (Tel: 982226) has 12 rooms.

RESTAURANTS

In the centre of Vila Baleira, the island's capital, is the Baiana bar-restaurant which specialises in local fare. On Ponta da Calheta, the Toca do Pescador serves excellent fish dishes. Near the airport, at Campo de Cima, is the Gazela Restaurant serving a variety of national and international dishes. The Theoderico is north-east of Vila Baleira in the hills of Serra de Fora and, due north is the 'Star of the North' restaurant for chicken specialities. In the far south of Porto Santo the Mariazinha, at Ponta, is well worth the short excursion from your hotel for their excellent local fish soups.

FOOD AND DRINK

The name of Madeira is famed throughout the world for its fortified wines and celebrated Madeira cake, but the islanders have many more delights to offer the gourmet. Surrounded by a bountiful sea which abounds in both warm and cold water fish, and with a land rich with fertile soil in which just about every imaginable vegetable and fruit thrives, the island has developed over five hundred years, a special culinary individuality.

Primarily Portuguese, Madeira has adapted the basic mainland menus and introduced flavours and tastes which combine those of the international kitchen with the local culinary arts. Visitors can take advantage of this *mélange* and select either exclusively Madeiran fare, which is generally simple and filling, or opt for foreign foods from the number of restaurants which cater for international tastes, or plump for a happy medium! The food on Madeira could not be fresher and the choice can be bewildering. It is useful to know a little about the variety of dishes found, not only in the dining rooms of the de-luxe hotels, but in the tiny village inns and guesthouses, or local country restaurants. The isle of Madeira offers a choice of more than forty little country restaurants either perched on the rocky coastline or set high on the terraced mountainsides and it is in these rural settings that the visitor might first savour the real tastes of Madeiran cookery.

MADEIRAN SPECIALITIES

The islanders generally adhere to what might be considered a rather limited diet and eat rather less meat than the Portuguese on the mainland. In many restaurants a single-course meal, known as *prato do dia* (chef's speciality of the day) will be advertised on a board at a set price. However, Madeirans supplement their main meals with fresh *saladas* (salads) and a wide variety of *frutas* (fruit). Commonly available foods include:

Fish : Peixe

bacalhau	cod (there is supposedly a different cod dish for each day of the year)
espadarte	swordfish
atun	tuna or tunny
carapau	mackerel
salmonete	red mullet
raia	skate
cherne	turbot
linguado	sole
perca	perch
truta	trout
robalo	sea bass
besugo	bream
sardinhas	sardines
enguia	eel
pescada	hake
peixe-espada	scabbard, cutlass fish (found in sea depths of over 6,000 feet – 2 kms. off the island shelf).

Shellfish : Mariscos

camarões	shrimp
gamba	prawn
vieras	scallops
amêijoas	cockle-size clam
langosta	spiny lobster
lagostin	crayfish
lavagante	deep-sea lobster
mexilhoes	mussels
ostra	oysters
caranguejo	crab
polvo	octopus
lulas	squid

Meat : Carne

bacon	bacon
chouriço	spicy sausage
almondegas	meatballs
presunto	smoked ham
frango	chicken
pato	duck
coelho	rabbit
codorniz	quail

perdiz	partridge
bife	steak
porco	pork
borrego	lamb
costeletas	chops
espetada	kebab
salsichão	salami
tora	special island sausage

Vegetables : Legumes

batatas	potatoes
cebola	onion
alho	garlic
arroz	rice
pepino	cucumber
tomates	tomatoes
alface	lettuce
beringela	aubergine – eggplant
pimentos	red and green peppers
couve	cabbage
cenoura	carrots
zucchini	courgettes
grão de bico	chick peas
inhame	sweet potatoes
bananas	savoury banana
ervilha	peas
feijãos	beans
azeitonas	olives
piripiri	African peppers

Fruit : Fruto

alperces	apricots
pêssego	peach
ananas	pineapples
toranja	grapefruit
roma	pomegranate
melão	melon
melancia	water melons
maça	apple
pêra	pear
ameixas	plums
morangos	strawberries
laranja	oranges
limão	lemons

limeira	lime
uvas	grapes
banana	banana

Nuts : Noz

amêndoas	almonds
amendoin	peanuts
avelãs	hazelnuts
nogueiras	walnuts
cajus	cashews
coco	coconut
castanas	chestnuts

TRADITIONAL DISHES

Possibly the most classic of all island fare – also the Portuguese national dish, is the *cozido à Portugesa*, a rich and substantial meat and vegetable stew with bacon, spicy sausage, beef, smoked ham, chicken, rice and a selection of vegetables including potatoes.

There are differences of opinion as to what might be called the typical Madeiran dish but making up one's mind between the delicious *caldeirada*, a tasty fish soup with potatoes and onions; *espedada da Madeira*, spit roasted chunks of beefsteak cooked over an aromatic fire made of laurel boughs; or the delicate, wine enhanced flavour of a uniquely Madeiran fish dish, the *peixe-espada* – a large and fearsomely ugly black creature found in the 6,000 feet (2 km.) depths off the island's coast, also known as the scabbard, or cutlass fish.

Other local fish dishes are:

bacalhau com todos cod cooked with a selection of vegetables including onions, garlic, olives and ovos (eggs) – literally cod with everything!

bif de atun tuna steaks are one of the delicacies of sub-tropical waters prepared with herbs and *limão* (lemon) over a charcoal grill.

ameijoas na cataplana A favourite island dish of small clam-like cockles, steamed with a selection of herbs and served with slices of sausages, (the cataplana is a copper saucepan-like container), or with cubes of marinated pork, known as '*carne de porco à alentajana*'.

Meat dishes are not as common as fish specialities and there are a few which might be unfamiliar like *coelho assado* – roasted rabbit, or *codorniz estufado* – stewed quail in wine. Rabbit, quail and partridge are all available during the October to December hunting season. Other meat dishes include *carne vinho e alho* – pickled pork and garlic, *sopa de coelho* – rabbit soup, *canja de galinha* – a chicken soup with rice, or *bife de cebolada* – beef simmered in wine with onions and spices.

Gaspacho   more commonly associated with Spain, this soup is an island delight. Served cold, it is made with cucumber, tomatoes, red and green peppers, onions and spices.

Caldo verde   another well-loved vegetable dish like a soup made with cabbage, potatoes and slices of the ubiquitous island sausage, *tora*, which seems to be added to most dishes!

Feijãos (beans) are a popular addition to stews and the many filling one-dish meals so typical of the island's fare. Chick peas are used to make either a bland soup or added to a meal as cus-cus. Another side-dish is made from *milho* (maize meal), or it can form the thickener in soups and stews. Maize flour is also made into a flat form of *pão* (bread) and maize cobs are often grilled over charcoal and added to any main course meal. Other garnishes include the inevitable *batatas frites* (fried potatoes), *inhame* (sweet potato) are also made into chips or crisps and the island's famous *bananas* (bananas) can be sliced and deep fried to make delicious snacks. *Azeite* (olive oil), as in mainland Portugal, is prevalent in most Madeiran cookery but *oleo* (corn oil) and *manteiga* (butter) is often used.

Desserts

Certainly better with a sip of excellent Madeira wine, the island's desserts are temptingly mouthwatering. *Bolo de caco* and *bolo de mel*, are the famous Madeiran honey cakes made with molasses, fruit, nuts and spiced with cinnamon. Rare treats to take home but undoubtedly one souvenir which will magically disappear before one boards the airplane or cruise liner! *Pudim de flan* is a popular sweet dish and consists of a custard cream caramel, topped with a Madeira sauce and served in a mould. Another dessert is *arroz doce* –

sweet rice, again made in a mould, the pressed rice has sugar and cinnamon spice added. An egg dish also made with sugar and spices, is *doces de ovos*. Most of the island's towns have a *pastelaria* (cake shop) where delicious pastries and cakes can be bought.

Finishing up the menu with brandy and coffee, one should know that *café* (coffee) comes in several forms – *bica*, small, strong, black; *galão*, very white in a glass; *garoto*, white coffee in a cup; *meia de leite*, a larger version of garoto and *carioca*, a little cup of diluted strong coffee.

Drinks

Banana and *açúcar* (cane sugar) crops are exported to boost the island's economy but sugar cane also contributes to a locally produced *cana* – rum which also goes into the local *poncha*, a fiery concoction of rum, honey and lemon. The local rum is known as *aguardente* and applies to most locally concocted cane sugar brews. The juice of sugar cane is also drunk as are those of many of the island's fruits.

The island's cherries contribute to the flavour of *grinjinha* – cherry brandy. *Anon* – sweetsop, *annona* – custard apples, *mango*, *papaya* – paw paw and guava are just a few of the more exotic fruits grown on the island and some of these fruits are used in the flavouring of *gelo* – ice cream. A special fizzy drink, *maracujá*, is made from the juice of the passion fruit.

Other beverages available on the island are the local *cerveja* – beer, 'Coral', rather a fine lager, imported beers and the Portuguese brandies and world-renowned ports.

Wine

Eight varieties of wine are imported from the mainland, Bucelas – an aromatic white wine; Carcavelos – both sweet and dry wines; Colares – red and white; Dão – yellow and red wines; Setubal – a muscatel; Vinhos Verdes – a dry, young, white and red wine; Pinhel – a rosé wine and the sparkling wines known as Vinho espumoso, or Bairrada, both red and white.

Madeira itself produces four main types of fortified wines for which it has a prodigious reputation built up over four hundred years. These varieties are Boal – a medium sweet aromatic wine; Malmsey – the most famous of Madeira's wine, full and strong, also called Malvasia; Sercial – dry and full-bodied wine and Verdelho – a dryish, russet-coloured wine. Madeira also produces several good table wines and all varieties are available, vinho branco – white wine; vinho tinto – red wine; vinho rosado – rosé wine; vinho clarete – light red, and vinho de mesa – table wine.

MADEIRA'S WINES

Madeira was almost created for the production of grapes. Vineyards line terraces on every mountainside, carpet valleys and even cling to cliffsides like strips of bright green paint against the dark volcanic rock. Both white and black grapes are grown on the island and Madeira's famous Malmsey and its Verdelho are made from the white, tinto is made from the black grapes. The celebrated wines of Madeira are produced under a special formula, dating back to the eighteenth century, which fortifies the wine by heating it over a period of three months in a unique process and then letting it cool slowly. This happens after a fermentation period in which the Sercial and Verdelho varieties are fermented completely dry and a grape spirit is mixed with the Boal and Malmsey types in order to enhance the sugar content. Sercial acquires the characteristics of a dry, nutty, Riesling wine as this is the area of Germany from which the vines were originally imported.

All the rest of Madeira's carefully selected grapes came from Candia (Crete) as a result of an edict issued by Prince Henry the Navigator during the first century of the island's discovery and imported by the Infante along with sugar cane from Sicily. Verdelho is the colour of golden amber and is one of the most popular wines for any occasion. Boal, a rich, aromatic wine, is the colour of yellow autumn leaves and is generally served after meals being the 'most balanced wine out of the Madeira stable'. For the finest, richest,

The wines which made Madeira famous

fullest and luscious variety one has to plump for Malmsey (the name of the vine), locally known as Malvoisie/ Malvasia. This succulent wine has all the attributes of a liqueur combined with the subtleties of the finest wines on earth. Only Madeira's sun, soil and its diligent people can produce such a thoroughly excellent drink which has gone down through the ages as the connoisseur's favourite. An ancient treaty between Portugal and England, concerning the importation of Port wine was drawn up in 1660 and a subsequent commercial pact was signed in 1703 giving the British a large share of the market which spread to include the Madeira wines.

Kings and princes clamoured for the privilege of sampling the unusual liquor and, it is related, the brother of King Edward IV of England, the Duke of Clarence, when incarcerated in the Tower of London on penalty of death, chose to be drowned in a 'butt of Malmsey' in preference to being beheaded. All this happened as far back as 1478 and, by 1597, Shakespeare had his hero, Falstaff, in *Henry VI*, exchanging his soul for ' ... a cup of Madeira and a cold capon's leg'. Around the same time both the island's wine and its sugar was so sought after that Flemish paintings and religious artifacts were exchanged for consignments of Madeira's precious produce.

Napoleon Bonaparte, sailing into Funchal in 1815 on his way to exile in St Helena, is said to have requested a cask of the precious liquor to savour during his final, lonely years on the South Atlantic island.

Madeira wines are a blend of the best of the island's produce of grapes from its carefully tended *poios*, or terraced vineyards. As early as the 1750s the improvement of wine which had been exported to the Indies and, part of it unsold, then returned to its port of origin, was noticed by discerning noblemen as having a unique flavour. Not only was the taste of the well-travelled wine enhanced, but the warmth of the passage to India and back, reacted on the wine in the barrels increasing its alcoholic strength. The process of warming and cooling the wine, now induced by an easier method than sending barrels on a round trip to the East Indies, is known as *estufagem*. Special rooms in the vineyards, called *estufas de calor*, are set aside for this secret process. During the *estufagem* small quantities of alcohol are added to the wine, fortifying the improving liquor. Once the effect of the new process on Madeiran wine became known, wine buyers of the eighteenth century descended on Funchal to buy this 'nectar of the Gods'. The wine known as Malmsey became the 'round trip from India' wine, or 'Round trip wine'.

MADEIRA'S WINES

During the harvest, which begins at the end of August, there are still parts of the island which celebrate the traditional method of handling grapes. In ancient times, once the grapes were harvested and crushed, because of the lack of easily negotiated roads, men used to transport grape juice to the estufas on their backs in 12-gallon goatskins. Today the old customs of wine production are still observed in some regions in order to preserve the tradition and those men who carry their precious liquid cargo are still known as *borracheiros*.

CELLAR TOURS

The names of Madeira's major wine-producing companies – Blandy's, Cossarts, Leacock and Miles, are part of the industry's fine and ancient heritage and the lodges (cellars) of the Madeira Wine Company, to which they belong, can now be visited. The Museum of the Madeira Wine Institute is well worth visiting at Rua 5 de Outubro. Next door to the Tourist Board Offices, at 28 Avenida Arriaga, opposite the São Lourenço Fortress in Funchal, guided tours take visitors around the premises, its interesting museum and cellars, ending with a tasting of Madeira's world-famous nectar.

For details of Madeira Wine Company tours Tel: 20 121.

PRACTICAL INFORMATION

TOURIST OFFICE

The Tourist Board in Madeira has four locations. It is called the Direção Regional de Turismo de Madeira, its main office is in Funchal at Av. Arriaga, 18. 9000 Funchal. Tel: 29057-25658. Tx. 72141 DTM FNC P.

At Santa Cruz the offices are located in the Airport of Santa Catarina, 9100 Santa Cruz. Tel: 52933. In Machico the address is Vila de Machico, 9200 Machico. Tel: 962712.

On Porto Santo the Posto de Turismo is in Vila Baleira, 9400 Porto Santo, Tel: 982361.

The Madeira Tourist Information Centres, under the auspices of the Portuguese National Tourist Offices are located in every major city in the world and, in the UK are at New Bond Street House, 1/5 New Bond Street, London W1Y 0NP. Tel: (01) 493 3873. In the USA the offices are at 548 Fifth Avenue, New York NY 10036-5089. Tel: (212) 354 4403-7.

CONSULATES

There are agencies for both British and American consulates in Funchal. The British Consulate agency is located at 14, Rua da Sé, Funchal. Tel: 21221. For US citizens the representation is at Avenida Luis Camões, Block D, Apartment B., Funchal. Tel: 47429.

BANKS AND CURRENCY

Banks are open from 8.30 a.m. until 11.45 a.m. and from 1.00 p.m. until 2.45 p.m. on weekdays. The currency on Madeira, the same as that in Portugal, is the Escudo. Shown as a $ sign, set between the units of escudos and centavos e.g. 10$50, ten escudo, fifty centavos. There are 100 centavos to the escudo and exchange rates of the escudo on the world market fluctuate. Most hotels have exchange facilities and the major credit cards are acceptable on the island as are traveller's cheques.

Tipping is customary and good service is usually rewarded at hotels, in restaurants and for taxi drivers or tourist guides.

POST AND TELEPHONE

Post Offices are known as CTTs, standing for Correios (mail), Telegrafos (telegrams) and Telefones (Telephones). The main Post Office is in Funchal on Avenida Zarco in the centre of town.

Telephones operate on a one escudo coin which is the cost of a local call but a telephone credit card system is also in use on the island and these can be bought at post offices where international calls can be made.

HEALTH AND MEDICAL CARE

A Medical Services Information Centre is at Rua das Pretas, 1, Funchal. This bureau provides helpful advice to visitors and tourists but, in an emergency, the telephone number for the ambulance service in Funchal is 29115 or 29116. Chemists are known as *farmacias* and stock most proprietary brands of medicines and the usual chemist's preparations.

There are no poisonous snakes or harmful creatures on Madeira but certain jellyfish and thornback rays should be avoided when swimming in the sea. The sun, however, can be more harmful than any land or sea creature and one should take the usual precautions against over-exposure to its deceptively innocuous rays.

ELECTRIC CURRENT AND WATER

The voltage on Madeira is generally 220v. A continental two-pin plug is used and adaptors are needed for most appliances brought to the island from Britain or the USA.

The water on Madeira is the freshest of mountain spring, water and that on Porto Santo is reputed to have health-giving properties. However, bottled water is available on the island.

RADIO, TV AND THE MEDIA

Satellite brings many continental radio and TV programmes to Madeira and there are three Portuguese language radio stations on the island. At times during the day a tourist programme is broadcast.

Many international newspapers and magazines are available on the island and there is an English language monthly publication called *Madeira Island Bulletin* which is often quite useful for visitors. The Tourist Board of Madeira sometimes stocks local information and specialist books.

TIME

Madeira is on Greenwich Mean Time and therefore the time remains the same as that in the UK. The island is five hours ahead of that in New York, i.e. midday in Madeira is 7 a.m. in New York.

PUBLIC HOLIDAYS

There are about twelve official *feriados*, or national public holidays celebrated on Madeira. In addition to these, the island enjoys a number of Saints' Days either locally in specific villages or across the island. The two-day carnival in February is one example of a semi-official Madeiran holiday.

January   New Year's Day is also celebrated with fireworks and parties. Often cruise liners stop over in Funchal for the beginning of year festivities adding to the exuberant atmosphere of *Ano Novo*.

New Year's Eve celebrations in Funchal harbour

February	Shrove Tuesday heralds Carnival and Good Friday observances follow.
April	Good Friday is observed and the Anniversary of the Revolution falls on 25 April.
May	Labour Day is celebrated on 1 May.
June	Corpus Christi Day falls during this month and Portugal's National Day – Cameons' Day is on 10 June.
August	The Day of Assumption falls on 15 August.
October	The Day of the Republic is celebrated on 5 October.
November	The festivities of All Saints' Day occur on 1 November.
December	The Restoration of Independence Day is remembered on 1 December and the Day of the Immaculate Conception falls on the 8th.

December — Natal, or Christmas Day comes in the middle of two weeks of celebrations and illuminations leading up to the New Year's Eve festivities.

On 31 December the main attraction on Madeira is the celebration of the Feast of St Sylvester in Funchal when the night sky is lit by a magnificent firework display.

See also local festivals under 'Culture and Folklore'.

CHURCHES

Roman Catholicism is the national religion of Portugal and therefore most of the churches on Madeira are Catholic and Mass is held regularly in almost every church including Funchal's Cathedral Sé, on Avenida do Dr Manuel de Arriaga. Anglican services are held in the English church on Rua de Quebra Costas in the capital.

SHOPPING

Shopping hours are from 9 a.m. until 1 p.m. and from 3 p.m.

till 7 p.m. On Saturday shops are only open during the morning until 1 p.m. The most natural souvenir of Madeira is a selection of its magnificent flowers. These, like the

Fine embroidery makes a lovely souvenir

spectacular Bird of Paradise flower, the island's famous orchids, or blooms of the Flamingo Flower, can be forwarded from the island, specially packed, to international addresses. Probably the best known local product of Madeira is its fortified wine, a bottle or two of which makes an excellent souvenir but check your duty-free limits!

The Portuguese, of course, are famed for their Port wine and an excellent brandy is also produced on the mainland. Malmsey, however, is the leader among drink souvenirs and the local liqueur, aguardente is a favourite buy.

Handicraft work is a speciality of the island and among the most attractive items are Madeira's exquisite embroidery work, its famous tapestries, highly-decorative inlaid woodwork items, wickerwork items from the cottage industries across the island, or carefully constructed wooden models.

The island's hand-painted tiles, in traditional blue and white designs, *azulejos*, are very popular and easy to pack, as are the pretty, coloured woollen dolls, or even dolls made of confectionery.

The island's women specialise in preparing delicious sweets and in preserving the exotic and succulent island fruits in syrup. Everyone has heard of the famous Madeira cake and this is an opportunity to sample the genuine article and perhaps take some home. Try the honey cake, the *bolo de caco* cake or a special treacle cake known as *bolo de mel*, which will probably get eaten before one reaches the airport or cruise ship. No matter, one of the local straw boater hats will show everyone where you've been!

Other, more bulky souvenirs include the island's artistic wrought-ironwork, hand-painted pottery and porcelain, a locally crafted guitar, or a *brinquinho* – a miniature model dance troupe in national costume attached to a short-sticked rattle, like an ornate tambourine. The islander's traditional boots, knee-length, but folded down to the ankle, make lasting souvenirs of a visit to Madeira.

PHOTOGRAPHY

Photographs are one way to share holiday experiences of the island and its charms and the local Madeirans are most obliging when it comes to taking pictures of flowersellers in national costume or the Funchal sledge-pushers launching couples down the city's cobbled slopes. However, a little

Portuguese used in the right way to request a photograph will be very appreciated. Try, *posso tirar una fotografia*. Most makes of film are available on the island but processing film locally is quite expensive. When taking a photograph remember that composition makes the difference between a good photograph and a snapshot. Frame the subject well, use trees, buildings, boats, and try different angles and unusual perspectives. Look for details in architecture, fishing boats, flowers etc. and get in close. Buy a few local postcards to show how a professional treats the scenic subjects and try to improve on these by varying the angles. Try to include people or activity in a photograph, it provides the focus even in photographs of comparatively uninteresting hillsides or buildings. The lighting conditions on Madeira make it an excellent location for good, clear photographs during the day. Don't forget that sunrise, sunset, and even moonlight, can produce unusual and effective results. Photographic experimentation and ingenuity make those memories even more rewarding.

GEOLOGY AND CLIMATE

ISOLATED GEMS OF THE OCEAN

Off the west coast of Africa, more than twenty million years ago, a clutch of little volcanoes sprouted up into the North Atlantic seas. Regularly throwing up molten lava and hot ash, deep-sea activity eventually transformed three groups of volcanoes into permanent islands which then suffered upheaval from the ocean floor and erosion from wind and sea. Today we know these tiny offshore clusters as the islands of the Azores, the Madeira Group and the Canary Islands.

The group which includes Madeira, evolved into mature islands with rocky surfaces surrounded, in the main, by high sea-cliffs and gouged on all sides by deep valleys and ravines. Two high plateaux were formed on the main island of Madeira and a long sandy beach built up on the south-east side of Porto Santo nearby. Mountain ranges cover both these islands and the highest peak on Madeira is Pico Ruivo de Santana (The Red Peak of Santana) at 6,106 ft; 1,861 m. On Porto Santo, Pico do Facho (Beacon Peak) stands 1,676 ft; 511 m. high but most of the island is a level plateau. Extinct volcanic craters and curious basalt formations exist on the main island which has the second highest ocean cliff in the world, Cabo Girão – a 1,933 ft; 589 m. drop almost vertically to the sea.

Madeira is really an archipelago consisting of one main island, Madeira itself (36 miles, 58 kms. in length and 14 miles, 23 kms. in width), Ilha do Porto Santo, a much smaller island (9 miles, 15 kms. long and 3 miles, 5 kms. wide) which lies 27 miles, 40 kms. to the north-east. To the south-west of Madeira are three almost uninhabited islands described in ancient charts as Ilhas Desertas – The Desert Isles. About 11 miles, 18 kms. of sea lies between Madeira and the three, Ilhéu Chão, Deserta Grande and Ilhéu de Bugio. More than 170 miles (275 kilometres) south of the main island are a group of isolated islets known as Ilhas Selvagens – The Savage Isles – which comprise of two principal and three tiny rocky outcrops which are rarely visited by anyone. This uninhabited group lies nearer to the Canary Islands but remains part of the Madeira archipelago.

The total area of the Madeira group of islands is around 308 sq. miles (797 sq. kms.) and the main island lies around 560 miles, 900 kms. south-west of Portugal's capital, Lisbon. The African coastline of Morocco is much nearer, just 435 miles (700 kms.) to the east of Madeira and the islands are on a similar latitude to that of Casablanca.

SUB-TROPICAL MODERATION

It is because of Madeira's southerly latitude that the island's climate is so mild throughout the year. Famous as a winter resort for visitors from northern Europe because January's temperature averages 60°F (16°C), the island's climate is equable all year round. In summer temperatures rarely rise above 75°F (23°C) and the Gulf Stream ensures that water temperatures range between 63°F (17°C) and 72°F (22°C).

Rain falls intermittently throughout the year but, during the summer – May to September – very little falls, and then mainly on the higher ground. Madeira can be cloudy in the summer afternoons but sunshine hours range from an average of six per day during winter and seven hours daily in summer. The sun, however, is much hotter than the average chart suggests as the sea breezes and exposed location of the island in the reflective seas of the Atlantic Ocean, combine with the unique micro-climate to create a real 'greenhouse' effect. It is wise to wear some sort of headgear, especially when hiking or walking long distances. When travelling in the mountains, however, the temperature can be quite chilly and, at times, turn really cold. It is best to be prepared for a considerable change in climate on a day's hike into the high, inland areas where valleys can be basking in bright sunlight but Madeira's famous peaks can be quite cool. Dusk is short-lived in these latitudes and so, if one is hiking in the mountains, it should be remembered that the sun sinks very rapidly.

The southern coast of the island is the warmest and, on the more exposed north coast, winds can sometimes be uncomfortably fresh. This particularly applies to visitors taking the boat trip to Porto Santo where one travels from the comparatively calm and sheltered south coast port of Funchal, out into the oceanic waters off the north coast.

The mountains around Faial

Despite the high humidity, the pleasant breezes off the Atlantic Ocean prevent any extreme climatic changes. Occasionally a warm wind blows off the Sahara far to the east, known as *L'este* from Africa, bringing a fine dust which disperses the clouds of evaporated sea water often seen around Madeira's high peaks. During August, one month that many visitors avoid, there can develop a wraith-like mist which obscures the sun and clings to the island for some weeks. This mist is known locally as the *capacete*.

Porto Santo is drier and even milder than its larger neighbour Madeira. With hardly any very high land the island usually escapes the 'halo' of cloud which often decorates the peaks of Madeira. This island often experiences droughts but the water that is found on Porto Santo is highly prized and a bottling plant supplies the health-giving water to the main island of Madeira.

For visitors from the cooler climates of Europe and America, the islands of Madeira never have a winter and therefore are a particularly attractive vacation destination in the winter months. The year-round climate maintains a constant average of 65° Farenheit or 18° Celsius although the humidity is generally quite high.

AVERAGE TEMPERATURES (FUNCHAL)

Month	Air F°	Air C°	Sea F°	Sea C °	Sun Hours
Jan	61	16	63	17	5.1
Feb	60	16	63	17	5.7
Mar	61	16	63	17	6.5
Apr	62	17	63	17	7.2
May	64	18	64	18	7.1
Jun	68	20	66	19	6.7
Jul	70	21	68	20	7.7
Aug	72	22	70	21	8.2
Sep	74	23	72	22	7.5
Oct	70	21	73	23	6.6
Nov	66	19	68	20	5.8
Dec	62	16	64	18	5.6

FLORA AND FAUNA

It is not known what Madeira looked like before Portuguese settlers set fire to the island in about 1420. Zarco, discoverer of both Porto Santo and Madeira, described the latter as densely forested, naming it the 'Isle of Wood'. Since then both the vegetation and wildlife had the opportunity to thrive practically unchecked on the ashes and embers of their forebears. Traces of the ancient forest which once covered the island can be seen occasionally. The unique Madeira ebony survives in the north of the island and the strange, primaeval dragon tree may have escaped the flames as it is also native to the nearby Canary Islands. Many seeds, tubers and roots must have lain dormant in the fire-baked soil even if the conflagration did last for the five years we are led to believe. Some species of pine, laurel, gorse and tree ferns, now prolific, can endure forest fires and certain cacti and succulents may have avoided extermination. In some isolated areas ancient vegetation such as trees over a thousand years old can be seen like the til tree, the dragon tree, some elderly cedars, the sesame and vinhatico, many dating before the years of island holocaust. Much of the vegetation of early times was the product of bird, sea, or windborne seeds and those trees and plants which were introduced for cultivation by early inhabitants.

Madeira's sub-tropical climate, fertile soil and sufficient annual rainfall provides ideal conditions for the propagation of almost any plant species on earth. It is for this reason that the island is now called 'The Flower of the Ocean' or 'The Floating Garden'. Whatever has been introduced to Madeira over almost six hundred years of settlement, has flourished and the island is now a botanical wonderland. Palm trees and bamboo are now commonplace as are yuccas, agave and even papyrus. Madeira was one of the first tropical lands to be cultivated by Europeans. The Portuguese brought their favourite vegetables, goats, pigs, sheep, cows, oxen, donkeys and ubiquitous pigeons with them as they established the island's first colony. Root crops and cereals thrived in the near-ideal environment as did the fruit trees which early settlers planted in their newly-acquired plots of land. Herbs and flowers also benefited from the perfect conditions, decorating the early village gardens and rivalling the expanses of wild flowers like the blue Pride of Madeira, purple heather and yellow meadow daisies.

It was not long before the first Madeirans began the introduction of major crops like sugar cane. Italians brought the sugar with them to Madeira as a jealously-guarded crop worth its weight in gold. First introduced in 1452, sugar cane became the island's leading crop and remains a major export to this day. Only once, in the late nineteenth century, did this hardy crop suffer from disease but a plant which was to change the fortunes of the islands once again was soon introduced, and this, the grapevine, was subject to severe attacks of blight and pest.

For centuries the wine of Madeira has won favour across the world and a local rum has traditionally been produced from the island's sugar cane. It is possible that Christopher Columbus' idea of taking sugar cane to the West Indies stemmed from his honeymoon days on Madeira and it was from his discoveries in the New World that mariners brought strange tropical fruits and flowers to add to the island's vegetation.

From the Portuguese discoveries in West Africa during the latter half of the fifteenth century, new plants and trees were introduced to Madeira and, by 1500, Amerigo Vespucci and Cabral had discovered South America on behalf of Portugal. Cabral had also journeyed from Lisbon to India and back. As a result of these expeditions the inhabitants of Madeira experimented with the first avocados, maize, sweet and soursop, pineapple, paw paw and passion fruit from the Americas and loquat, cherries, spices and herbs from the East Indies. Captain Cook, visiting the island twice during the late eighteenth century, remarked on Madeira being the '... recipient of Nature's most liberal gifts'. It is possible that he brought with him several botanical gifts from the south seas like the poinsettia which now grows here in profusion, the silk oak from Australia, eucalyptus and mimosa.

Today the flora of the island reads like a botanist's tour of the world. Hydrangeas, magnolias and rhododendrons from the east; coral trees, franciscia, golden trumpet, jacaranda and bougainvillea from South America; tree heather and the red hot poker from Ethiopia; the belladonna lily, agapanthus and podranea from South Africa; the red-leaved

The familiar banana plant was introduced to Madeira in 1842

Nanha de Pascoa comes from Central America and the brilliant hibiscus originated in China. The island is a wealth of bloom, both familiar and strange. Begonias vie for space with camellias, frangipani grow alongside the African flame trees, geraniums grow next to fuscias, bougainvillea drapes over balconies along with wisteria, the cork tree dwarfs the carob bush and the odd kaffir bean tree shades garden plots where English roses bloom. Curiously-named species like the flamboyant flamingo flower and the magnificent bird of paradise bloom, the *orqidea de haste*, and the exotic madonna, or white lily grow in carefully cultivated masses for export.

Madeira might well be called the 'Fruit Basket of the World' because of the variety of species which thrive under its sub-tropical sun. Bananas are an important export crop and the island's famous grapes provide the world with the celebrated vinho generoso and Malmsey wines. Apples and pears, strawberries and plums, apricots and peaches from temperate climates grow in the same fertile soil as the oranges, lemons, grapefruit, almonds, chestnuts, hazelnuts and figs of Mediterranean shores. More exotic are the passion fruit from South America which provide a drink known as Maracuja, the guava, papaya and custard apple from the Caribbean. Sweet sop and mangoes drip from trees in the same orchards as the avocado tree and pineapple plants and in the 'poios' or agricultural terraces melons tangle round the trunks of medlar trees. All manner of vegetables are cultivated in garden plots or mountainside terraces.

WILDLIFE

Wildlife is limited on the Madeiran islands although many species of migratory birds use these isolated landfalls on their Atlantic wanderings. On Governor Perestrello's first voyage to his domain of Porto Santo, we are told, he imprudently brought a number of rabbits, probably to keep down the rampant vegetation. Unfortunately it was the rabbits which adopted a characteristically rampant nature and the island has been plagued by infestations of the creatures ever since! Today, rabbits are culled during the hunting seasons from October to December. Partridge and quail are also prevalent on this rocky island and sea-birds claim the shoreline cliffs and sandy beaches. Although the small island of Porto Santo escaped the flames which wrought havoc on Madeira's forests, it is comparatively barren and supports little more than palms and the vegetation of a typical arid climate.

The far-off Ilhas Desertas, south-east of Madeira, have been designated a wildlife reserve for their profusion of sea-birds. These islands are also famous for their wildlife as Europe's largest arachnid, the wolf spider, haunts these islands. Also given the name wolf, and also regular visitors to the 'Desert Isles', are the seals which play around the coasts of these three barren outcrops.

On Madeira itself, there are no large numbers of domesticated animals to be seen because the terrain is so craggy and treacherous. Livestock, particularly cattle, are kept in thatched byres. Some sheep can be seen wandering on pasture land on the plateaux and on valley floors, and goats and pigs are also reared. Cattle are free to graze on the sparse vegetation of Porto Santo as the island is comparatively flat. Also on the smaller island, donkeys are used as beasts of burden, an animal hardly seen on mountainous Madeira. In discoverer Zarco's time the 'sea wolves' or seals, were common around Madeira's south coast and mariners named one promontory *Câmara de Lobos* – 'Wolf Lookout' because of the creatures which were often seen there. Other authorities put the origin of the village's name down to the sea perch, once known as 'wolf-fish' which congregated in the waters off this bay. Today there are still groups of seals which can be spotted around the island's rocky shores.

Butterflies, frogs, lizards and rabbits more-or-less complete the Madeira island's roll call of wildlife but what it lacks on its islands it gains in its harvest from the sea. The deep Atlantic Ocean surrounding Madeira abounds in fish – cod, mackerel, sea bass, red mullet, bream, turbot, plaice, hake, sole, skate, sardines and conger eel. Sportsfishermen catch bigeye, bluefin and longtail tuna, dorado, bonito, amberjack, blue marlin, swordfish, tunny, hammerhead, porbeagle, thresher and blue shark. Shellfish litter the shallow pools around its shores – lobster, crayfish, crabs, prawns, shrimps, scallops, oysters, mussels and clams. Around the rocky cliffs squid, octopus and cuttlefish are taken and, in the island's streams and rivers fishermen try for trout, which are framed on the island, and for carp.

LEVADAS AND POIOS

Once streams, rivers, fountains and waterfalls gushed down the steep mountain slopes of Madeira, washing the precious topsoil to the sea and creating deep clefts and gullies in the volcanic rock. The backbone of mountains running from east to west of the island broke rainclouds brought by the prevailing north-east winds and much of the precipitation fell on the north side of Madeira leaving the south side dry for many months.

Without many other natural resources except land and water, the problem for early settlers was to improve the lot

LEVADAS AND POIOS

Madeira's agricultural terraces, or 'poios'

of the land and consequently their own. Having exploited the island's few low-lying areas of cultivatable land on flat clifftops, pastures nestling in steep-sided valleys and the rich soil clinging to the hillsides in the south of the island, Madeirans resorted to shaping the remaining available land to their needs. Over centuries the islanders toiled to tame the wild mountainsides.

In the very early days both slave and convict labour was used to transform the rugged landscape. Terraces, called *poios* were cut into the rocky slopes and flat areas for agricultural crops were carved from cliff faces. In wicker baskets strapped to their backs, the farmers transported soil up steep mountainsides to these laboriously engineered terraces. The terrain in Madeira has always been too steep for donkeys or horses to negotiate and even cattle are kept penned on flat plots to prevent them falling over the steep cliffs surrounding farm plots. The pens, known as *palheiros* are thatched sheds, and the cattle are taken outside just for exercise and fresh air.

Channelling the plentiful supply of spring, stream and river water to follow man-made routes around their newly claimed plots, leading to watercourses along flat terraces and even tunnelling them through mountainsides, the Madeiran farmers devised ways of making the fullest use of the water before allowing it to cascade into the sea. So important was the organisation of these water tracts to the island's economy that, as far back as the late 1400s official legislation was outlined to assign water rights to farmers. By the turn of the last century there were around two hundred waterways completed. These channels, culverts and aqua-ducts form a pattern across the rugged landscape and are known as *levadas*. Irrigating the precious soil – only around one-third of the land surface of Madeira is cultivatable – required courage, determination and tenacity. Some of these waterways follow precarious courses where one could not imagine their constructors working. Precipitous cliffs drop away below lovingly-built watercourses and narrow pathways hug the carefully cut channels around towering mountains and hillside terraces.

Today more than 1,300 miles (2,000 kms.) of *levadas* now exist across the island, some with spectacular waterfalls, some cutting through dense woodland and 25 miles (40 kms.) of waterway burrowing through hillsides in order to keep the thousands of terraces watered. These *levadas*, a miracle of early engineering, form a network, not only of waterways feeding the precious *poios*, but of pathways along which workers and visitors alike can traverse the mountain-ous hinterland of Madeira. Cutting deep across mountain ranges, following the contours of wooded hills and weaving in and out of steep-sided valleys, the *levadas* provide a most original way for the energetic to explore the island's countryside. About twenty of the more easily negotiable *levadas* offer the hiker the freedom to walk deep into the island's interior with the accompanying pleasure of con-stantly cool and gurgling water alongside their path.

Around Funchal, the Levada do Curral diversifies from great cavernous tunnels carved into solid basalt to valley-hugging garden scenes and pretty settings with woodland and farmhouses. Together with the Levada dos Piornais with its ocean views it is a popular excursion and whets the appetite for some of the more rigorous and demanding levada walks to the west, north and central parts of the country. In the centre of the island, above Funchal, is the Levada dos Tornos with its tiny, thatched, levada-side cottages and ancient orchards; in the high, Paul da Serra range of mountains are the Levada das Vinte e Cinco Fontes, the 'levada of twenty and five falls' and the Levada do Paúl; in the north are the *levadas* of Inferno and Faja Rodrigues and the famous Levada do Norte through the Água mountains with its dramatic scenery. To the west is the great Levada da Central da Ribeira da Janela. Far in the east of the island a favourite walk is along the Levada

LEVADAS AND POIOS

Machico-Canical, with its green-carpeted terraces and little red-tiled cottages.

It is really on these *levada* walks that one can truly experience the earthy nature of the island and appreciate the great lengths to which the islanders have gone to bring fertility and prosperity to their beautiful island. Madeira's great variety of trees, flowers and crops can be enjoyed from the canalside pathways which open up this delightful island to the sensitive visitor. Some of the walks are more difficult, some can be real hikes and some require effort on the part of the hiker, both to find and navigate, but it is the explorer, the inquiring and the discriminating traveller who will benefit from these spectacular walkways which open up the interior to aficionados of the island, its people and its unique scenery.

HISTORY, ECONOMY AND INDUSTRY

A MYSTERIOUS FLOATING FOREST

No evidence has ever been found of very early habitation on any of the Madeira archipelago islands as is the case on the nearby Canary Islands. Certainly there was a profusion of life as the island was covered in a thick forest which dated back to prehistoric times. Even today there are remnants of this vegetation in the great tree ferns and ancient dragon trees. It was not until around 1000 BC that the group was first mentioned in history. Before this no civilisation had touched the isolated Atlantic islands. The Phoenicians first discovered the islands as they traded beyong the 'Pillars of Hercules' and down the West African coast. Phoenician merchants may have introduced the art of producing a purple dye, for which they were famous, to the islands because they were known as *Insulae Pururiae* (The Purple Isles) during the first century BC in the reign of King Juba II of Mauritania. The Greek philosopher Plato's mythical Atlantis was said to be located in the region of Madeira and, in the second century AD the Egyptian geographer Ptolemy apparently included the islands on his famous map of the known world. However, since then, nothing was heard of these forgotten isles for over a thousand years and it is a complete mystery how these islands were 'lost' for such a long time.

ABANDONED BY THE ANCIENTS – REDISCOVERED BY MISTAKE

Legends persist on Madeira of an Englishman named Robert Machim, who, fleeing either the wrath of a rival in love, or the ravages of the Plague, sailed south from Bristol with his mistress, Anna d'Arfet. The year has been identified as about 1348 and a sudden storm, it is said, drove their craft onto the deserted island of Madeira. The couple survived the ordeal only to expire weeks afterwards of exposure. Crewmen from the wreck buried the couple under a tree and sailed from the island in a makeshift raft.

The palms remind visitors that they are in the tropics

Captured by Moorish pirates, the sailors told their story in Morocco and, eventually it reached the ears of King John I of Portugal as he led his army against the pirate haunt of Ceuta. The King related the tale of Machim to his young sons including Henry, later to be called Henry the Navigator. Prince Henry, fired by his father's tale, was just 25 years old when he instructed two of his naval commanders to lead an expedition around the west African coast in search of this lost island. João Gonçalves Zarco and Tristão Vaz Tiexeira were despatched on the mission in a 'não' of the prince's design. Sailing south the voyagers were driven by a fierce storm onto the coast of the island of Porto Santo in 1418. In the distance the sailors noted a large cloud which remained in one place on the horizon. The Portuguese navigators speculated that the cloud's position might indicate an unexplored land. Inquisitive, but anxious to get news of Porto Santo back to Portugal, the explorers were not to return to discover the larger island until the following year.

When Zarco and Tiexeira eventually landed on Madeira it was in exactly the same bay that the English couple had been shipwrecked just seventy years before. A grave was found, or so the tale goes, in which Machim and his lover were discovered. Today the name of Machim survives in the little fishing port of Machico, on Madeira's east coast. The island, Zarco relates, was covered by a dense forest and the captain immediately dubbed it 'Ilha da Madeira' – 'Isle of Wood'. On returning to Lagos in Portugal, Prince Henry apportioned out the newly-discovered to three governors who were charged to develop the island. Zarco received an area of land around what is now the capital, Funchal; his companion, Tiexeira, was allocated Machico and the rest of the island; and another governor, Bartolomeu Perestrello de Moniz, was given the island of Porto Santo. Zarco's men began to clear the trees in order to construct the island's first settlement. Fire seemed to be the quickest solution to the problem of preparing land for building and agriculture. The favourable winds which now make the island's climate so pleasant, fanned the settler's flames, setting fire to the entire island. Eye-witnesses said that Madeira burned for five, or even seven years – a baptism by fire. From the ashes of that holocaust rose a green phoenix which must now be even more beautiful than the forested land Zarco first sighted.

SEVEN YEARS OF CONFLAGRATION – THEN SETTLEMENT

From the safety of his own island, Perestrello must have watched Madeira burn but he had his own problems in the form of the rabbits which he had introduced onto Porto Santo. A plague of rabbits almost cleared the land of vegetation as successfully as the fire had done on the larger island! The year was 1420, but it was not until five years

The old section of Funchal

later than settlement began in earnest on Madeira. By 1425, Zarco had built a chapel in Funchal, the capital town which he named after the surrounding banks of fennel. It is said that the first children to be born on Madeira were twins named Adam and Eva, and that a tiny chapel was erected in Funchal to commemorate the event. Zarco lived as governor of his part of the island for 42 years. In 1452, the introduction of sugar cane, a crop which thrived in the sub-tropical climate and was known in Europe as 'white gold' because of its value, brought prosperity to Madeira. Italian farmers had shown the Portuguese how to cultivate sugar and also grapevines, introduced from Crete, were soon being grown on the island's terraces and Madeira's famous wine production began. Numbers of African slaves were brought from Morocco to work in the cane fields. A chapel was built in 1470 on the site of the English grave of Machim in the town which holds his name and, in 1479, Christopher Columbus sailed into Funchal harbour on a trading mission to buy a quantity of sugar. That same year Columbus married the governor of Porto Santo's daughter, Felipa Isabel Moniz Perestrello, and settled for a short time on the island, moving to reside in Funchal in 1479. Thirteen years later Columbus sailed west to discover the Americas having studied navigation during his stay on Madeira.

PLAGUE, PIRATES, PROSPERITY

The Sé Cathedral in Funchal was begun in 1485 and King Manuel gave Funchal a Charter in 1508 when the town took on city status. The island prospered – apart from two outbreaks of the Plague in 1523 and 1538. The capital had been left in peace for more than 140 years from the time it was established until, in 1566, the French pirate Bertrand de Montluc, swept into the tiny port with three ships. Ransacking the city and creating havoc on the island for more than two weeks, Montluc left the islanders to lick their wounds for another 12 years. In 1580 Portugal, along with Madeira and the Azores, came under Spanish rule which was to last for sixty years. Spanish colonists built a number of churches and forts on the island and returned Madeira to Portugal in 1640. During 1660 a treaty of commerce was signed between the island and Britain which developed the wine trade. Special dispensations also, were made to all Englishmen settling on Madeira in 1662, when King Charles II married the Portuguese Princess Catherine de Braganza, although he unwisely declined to accept the island of Madeira as part of the wedding dowry. The Spanish, however, ignored any special favours and ties between Madeira and Britain which had existed for almost three hundred years, not acknowledging the independence of Portugal until six years later in 1668. Exactly a hundred years later Captain Cook, in his ship *Endeavour*, came to collect botanical specimens on Madeira, returning for more examples in 1772. Cook probably also left some exotic species on Madeira for the islanders to cultivate themselves.

The important position of Madeira on the Atlantic trading routes proved very attractive to English merchant fleets and a strong tie grew up between the two islands. Many English people settled in Madeira's favourable climate of prosperity and warmth and the wine trade especially flourished. During the Napoleonic Wars British troops occupied Madeira in order to protect both Portuguese and English interests. Twice in 1801 for six months, and in 1807 for seven years the British army was garrisoned on the island and many soldiers became romantically attached to the island's attractive girls, staying on as residents after the troops returned to England in 1814. The British military presence was based in three villages on the island, Camacha, Monte and Santa da Serra. The alliance formed between the two countries, 600 years ago – 16 June 1373, is said to be the oldest in the world. The following summer, on the way to his exile in St Helena, Napoleon Bonaparte passed through the port of Funchal.

In the early 1840s British merchants introduced a speciality of banana to the island from Demerara.

One famous English name in Madeira during Victorian times was that of Miss Elizabeth Phelps who introduced, in 1856, a commercial aspect to the traditional art of embroidery practised on Madeira. About this time Madeira began to attract tourists from all over Europe, but particularly from Britain. Blight disease damaged the entire Madeiran vineyards during 1852 and a cholera epidemic hit the islands in 1856. Again the vines on the island were annihilated by pests during 1873 and the sugar crop was decimated in 1882.

RELUCTANTLY INTO THE TWENTIETH CENTURY

Madeira was granted the status of a Republic within Portugal in 1902 and later established an internal self-government. For 14 years Madeira slept in peace under the semi-tropical sun until World War I broke out, and even then she seemed miles from the hostilities. However, in 1916, a German submarine crept into Funchal harbour, sinking three Allied ships, returning the next year to demonstrate the kaiser's influence by lobbing several shells into the city's dockside area. The anchor chains from the friendly ships which went down in the attack now adorn the monument to peace above the harbour of the capital. Madeira suffered a semi-siege during the last years of the First World War.

Madeira has witnessed a number of miracles during its five-hundred-year history and, during 1917, another appearance of Our Lady of Fátima underlined the religious devotion of the people of the island.

Retiring from political life in Europe, the last Austro-Hungarian emperor, Karl I (Charles IV of Hungary), and his wife, the Empress Zita, made their home on Madeira during 1918. It was 1921 when a seaplane first made a successful flight from Lisbon to the island and, the following year, in 1922 the Emperor Karl died and was buried on the island at Monte. The market in Funchal was constructed in 1941. A regular, experimental commercial seaplane link from Portugal was established in 1949. It was not until 1960 that an airfield was opened on the islands, and then it was built on Porto Santo but, by 1964 Madeira had its own airport and tourists began to flock in.

GREAT NAMES AND
A GRAND FUTURE

The natural products of Madeira have been enjoyed by the world's élite. The world's most celebrated discoverer, Columbus, chose the balmy air and magnificent scenery (plus the company of a local lass) for his honeymoon. An Emperor and his Empress selected Madeira as their retirement home, the famous Captain Marryat and Captain James Cook both waxed lyrical about the island's natural attractions, Sir Winston Churchill chose the island for his relaxing artistic holidays, the French king François I developed a sixteenth-century liking for Madeira's famous wine and Admiral Lord Nelson had a particular penchant for the delicious nectar. In the Tower of London, some contemporary accounts allege that the Duke of Clarence preferred to die by drowning in a butt of Malmsey rather than by beheading!

Today thousands of discerning visitors arrive to enjoy the island's delights either by air, or from the many cruise liners which regularly put in to Funchal harbour. Tourism is now a major part of the island's economy and holidaymakers enjoy, not only the spectacular scenery, but sports like fishing, golf, riding, walking, tennis, sailing, scuba diving and other watersports. Beaches, particularly on Porto Santo, rocky bays and pools attract water-lovers and sunbathers whilst sightseers enjoy the historic surroundings and the verdant countryside. For night life there is a casino and

A major tourist development at Matur, near the airport

Funchal's western shoreline

Madeira's capital, Funchal, surrounds the bay

The art of embroidery has been handed down over the ages

Porta da Cruz on the rugged north-east coast

View from the world's second highest ocean cliff – Cabo Girão

Porto Santo's tiny capital of Vila Baleira

The traditional method of transporting wine

Near Porta da Cruz is the famous *Penha d'Águia* or 'Eagle Rock'

A government-run Pousada, Vinháticos

Funchal's Botanical Gardens

Câmara de Lobos – a favourite subject
for Winston Churchill's paintbrush

Traditional dancing

A beautiful hibiscus, typical of Madeira's
exotic flowers

Hedgerows burst with bloom throughout most of the year

several nightclubs in which to relax. The travel industry also brings in foreign currency from the sale of the island's varied souvenirs. Apart from the world-famous wines and Madeira's limitless supply of exotic flowers and fruits, craft articles are also sought after such as the delicate embroidery – a local trade now employing some 30,000 women throughout the islands – tapestries, porcelain, glassware, woollen items, wickerwork, or handicrafts such as carved models of the traditional sailing craft.

Funchal port lies on several important shipping routes and is a stop-over for commercial freighters. The islands also have their own trade with Europe and more distant destinations. Being a major supplier of fresh fruit and vegetables, wine and flowers, sugar and fish, the island's exports comprise pineapples, bananas, apples, pears, plums, custard apple, guavas, loquat, oranges, lemons, mango, paw paw, passion fruit, melons and avocados. Madeira also contributes to Portugal's status as the world's seventh largest wine producer.

CULTURE AND FOLKLORE

With less than six hundred years of history and being situated in such an isolated location it is difficult to imagine Madeira having as rich a tradition as most European countries. However, being positioned on Europe's strategic trade and exploration routes and having benefited from the skills of a variety of settlers, Madeira developed its own special traditions. The influx of sects, cults and religions from as far away as Northern Europe, and as near as Morocco instilled a mixed range of festivals and observances, evolving a deep Roman Catholic religious conviction. Evidence of this is seen in the numerous chapels, churches and shrines dotted across the island. Madeiran architecture particularly demonstrates the diverse influences which have contributed to the island's culture. Out of necessity, technical skills, like the construction of the levadas, or irrigation channels, changed the landscape and the levelling of poios, or terraces on Madeira's mountainsides, wrested what arable land could be gained from the rocky terrain.

Formal gardens, laid out later by the owners of Quintas, or grand country mansions, were designed in a specially terraced manner in order to accommodate the inclines of this hilly island. In the towns the Madeirans cobbled their steep streets and even the sled vehicles were especially designed to cope with the uneven terrain. Often transport of the elderly, or invalid, was engineered by special hammocks and the islanders designed wicker baskets to carry field produce, building materials and even children on their backs because of the steep tracks. In the countryside, farmers and vineyard workers created their own particular style of dwelling. This was an acutely angled, thatched roof over an almost wall-less house with brightly painted shuttered windows at the front and back and with a wicker-fenced garden. Unchanged to this day, these quaint, thatched cottages are still constructed and the islanders' cattle are kept in byres known as *palheiros*, built along the same design.

A colourful national costume has evolved on the island which includes a little dark cap with red flashes for the

Typical thatched housing in the Santana region

women, with white blouse, highly embroidered waistcoat, brightly striped full skirt and scarlet bolero cape. Since a 1933 declaration, women flower sellers are required to wear the island's national costume by law. The men wear a woolly cap with a bobble called a *carapucha*, black, or white linen waistcoat and trousers, red cumberbund and bright neckscarf. Both men and women wear the traditional soft leather boots, or *botacha*, knee-high, but worn rolled down to the ankles. Other versions of local costume are also worn, particularly during feast days or festivals. Most dances and folklore performances relate to life on the land and re-enact certain agricultural duties in ritual such as the Heavy Dance in which the imaginary trading of grapes is included. This dance is accompanied by music more typical of African than of Europe and is a throwback to the days of slavery on Madeira.

Another dance associated with the wine industry is that known as the Carrier's Dance where the men cavort with baskets loaded with imaginary grapes. Slave workers are again symbolically remembered in a popular dance known as the dance of the Ponta do Sol, an area where most of Madeira's slaves were housed. Many other traditional dances can be seen on the islands as folkloric troupes visit hotels and give performances on tours and at annual festivals.

The music accompanying island dancing is as mixed in origin as its performers and several of the more popular

Traditional music and dancing

instruments include the *machête* – producing a guitar-like sound, another, four-stringed guitar-like instrument known as a *braguinha*, the *brinquinho* – like a miniature maypole around which little national costumed dolls spin and which produces a metallic rattle, and the *rajao* – another curious stringed instrument, all unique to the island. Mandolin, accordion, viola, drum and triangle join in the ancient medleys and produce a haunting sound with European, African and Moorish overtones. The most popular music of the islands, and of Portugal, is the *Fado*, or Fate Song, a traditionally melancholy and plaintive story put to music, generally with a moral or tragic theme. As well as regular folk-dancing demonstrations, Madeira is an island which revels in its many festivals and religious feasts. It is at these celebrations that the spirit of the people, their exuberant nature and colourful costumes come to the fore. There are many local fêtes or pilgrimages held in the rural villages throughout the year and these are known as *romarias*.

Other important festivals, fifteen in all, include:

February	The Island's Carnival
April	The 3-day Flower Festival
June	The 8-day Bach Festival and a day-long

	Sheep Shearing Event also the São Joao da Ribeira's Festival in Funchal and the Festival of San Pedro in Ribeira Brava.
August	The Madeira Wine Rally and the Festa da Sĕnhora do Monte.
September	The Grape Harvest Festival and the waterborne procession in Caniçal on the Festival of Nossa Sĕnhora da Piedade. Also the local feasts of Sĕnhor Jesus in Ponta Delgada, the feast of Nossa Sĕnhora do Loreto in Calheta and that of Nosso Sĕnhor dos Milagres held in Machico.
October	The burning of the bonfires in the S.S. Sacremento Festival celebrated in Machico.
December	Two weeks of Christmas celebrations and, on New Year's Eve The grand Festival of Madeira (Festas de São Silvestre).

Flowers proliferate throughout the celebrations on Madeira as do the traditional flags – a red cross on a white ground, recalling the sails of discoverer Zarco's ships.

See 'Public Holidays' section for full list of official holidays.

ISLAND CRAFTS

WICKERWORK

With a wooded, mountainous island, comparatively isolated from mainland Portugal, Madeiran people resorted to improvising housing, tools and utensils from the national resources around them. Reeds served to thatch the early 'wattle and daub' houses and wooden runners were made for carts and wagons which would not negotiate the steep island tracks if fitted with conventional wheels. Most of the hillside paths were too narrow and tortuous for horses, donkeys or other beasts of burden and so the people of the island were compelled to carry everything themselves. Large baskets were made to strap on the carriers' backs and goatskins were used to transport liquids. Chairs and tables, baskets and boxes were fashioned from the willow osiers which grew along the banks of Madeira's network of levadas, or irrigation channels. Even today, the art of weaving willow wands can be seen in Madeira and particu-

Osiers stacked for the homecraft of wickerwork

larly in the mountain town of Camancha.

The thin willow reeds are first cut, peeled, dried and then stored for use. It is a common sight across the island to see clumps of willow reeds leaning against cottage walls or even stacked on roofs in bundles drying, before being made supple by a lengthy boiling in special troughs to make them flexible enough to work. Along the *levada* banks, the weird stumps of willow trunks show where the wickerworker has cut the materials for his craft.

The art of weaving the willow wicker into all sorts of household items has placed Madeira on the map as one of the foremost sources of wickerwork in the world. Today these trays, bottle baskets, trugs, picnic baskets, stools and even chairs, are sought-after souvenirs of the ancient handwrought craft. Almost a thousand different items are produced from this cottage industry which is an important export-earner for the island.

EMBROIDERY

A disaster in the vineyards of Madeira was said to be responsible for another of the island's famous crafts. In 1852 a small beetle, phylloxera, decimated the grapevines across the land and brought near economic ruin to Madeira. Many thousands of workers were out of employment, including hundreds of women. A Victorian Englishwoman, Miss Elizabeth Phelps, the daughter of a wine importer, visited the pest-wracked island in 1856, and noticed the fine embroidery work created by the women who were without work.

Such was the praise for Madeiran embroidery in England, that Miss Phelps returned to the island and began organising the women into communal groups of workers, selling their work for charity and so saving the plight of the former vineyard workers. The scheme was successful and now the island's cottage industry employs thousands of groups of women all over the island, stitching away in, workshops and on rural terraces. Quality is rigorously maintained by the Instituto do Bordado and embroidery is now one of the island's most important exports and a favoured souvenir for visitors. Designs are hand-embroidered after the *broderie anglaise* fashion on Irish linen, lawn, organdie cotton, cambric and even silk. Tablecloths, bedcovers, handkerchiefs, dresses, sheets, shirts, blouses and a hundred other items are on sale in shops like the Casa Oliveira, on Rua da Alfandega, Funchal, where workshops can be viewed, or in the island's street-markets. The Instituto do Bordado is at Rua Visconde de Anadia, Funchal.

TAPESTRY WORK

The Madeirans have had a long tradition of trading and working with the Flemish people and the skill of weaving tapestries probably dates back to those times when the Flemish began exchanging valued paintings and art treasures for the island's produce, particularly sugar. The art of tapestry work was considered so important that, in 1780, a decree was issued to support the craft. Even before embroidery became an important island handicraft, tapestries were exhibited as an integral part of the Madeiran industry in the 1850 International Fair. Dedicated to preserving this ancient skill, two Germans, Max and Herbert Kiekenben, developed the craft into a profitable concern in 1936.

Most of the *petit point* and tapestry designs are copies of the Flemish religious works of art, reproductions of famous paintings and original Madeiran designs emanating from the islander's environment. A variety of souvenirs are woven and these include such household items as wall coverings, rugs, cushions, bedspreads, chair coverings and handbags. The Instituto do Bordado also protects the fine quality of this distinctive folk art. One shop which specialises in Madeiran tapestries is Brasao e Freitas on Rua do Conselheiro, Funchal.

OTHER ISLAND CRAFTS

The hand-painting of tiles, traditionally with designs in blue glaze on white – hence their name *azulejos* – is an ancient craft derived from Spain and the Moors in the sixteenth

ISLAND CRAFTS

century. This art form remained on the Portuguese main-land before arriving in Madeira around the latter part of the seventeenth century. The classically ornate tiles were used for cladding exterior and interior surfaces, creating pictures and edging windows and doorways with a running frieze of tiles. Churches, chapels and estate houses were decorated with the ceramic tiles which provide both a protection and an aesthetic ambience to plain surfaces. *Azulejos* are now a sought-after craftwork as souvenirs of the island. Most examples of the *azulejo* tiles available on Madeira now manufactured in factories in Portugal.

Exquisite inlay work, marquetry and carved wooden items are fashioned by Madeiran craftsmen. Colourful cockerels, model fishing boats of wood and a selection of pottery, porcelain and glassware items are created for the tourist trade as souvenirs of the island. Woollen items like rugs and bedspreads are woven as a cottage craft and straw and rushes are plaited into boater hats and household goods. Many of the objects crafted on the island are especially manufactured for the tourist trade and, as a large percentage of islanders live in isolated farms, their craftwork gives them an opportunity to make a profitable living.

LEISURE AND SPORT

Many visitors come to the Madeira islands to enjoy the leisurely way of life and relax in the languid atmosphere around swimming pools, rocky bays or the sandy beaches of Porto Santo. Other visitors prefer to stroll in the botanic gardens or take a tour to view the historic sites, museums and churches. Demanding little or no exercise on the part of the visitor are the special toboggan rides in wickerwork sleds on wooden runners (*carros de cesto*), in which local 'drivers' in straw boaters propel the riders down the steep, shiny, cobbled lanes of Funchal. Alternatively, bullocks, or oxen pull larger sledges around the streets. Once this was part of their everyday work but now the sleds act as sightseeing vehicles for the enjoyment of tourists.

WALKING AND HIKING

Another popular relaxation in these islands is the opportunity to stroll comfortably around the terraced villages and hillside woods taking a peaceful pleasure in the delights of the island's natural attractions. Some prefer a more strenuous activity like long mountain hikes which can be made along the intricate irrigation system (*levadas*) on Madeira. These paths take the walker high up into the island's interior and through canal tunnels (*furados*) in the rocks providing rewarding vistas of Madeira's spectacular countryside. The Tourist Board has all details of organised excursions or maps and advice for independent walkers and hikers.

HORSE RIDING

A little more adventurous are those visitors who take advantage of the horse riding tours available from the Centro de Hipismo de Madeira, Caminho dos Pretos. Rides take place every weekday from 9.30 a.m. to 5 p.m. Tel: 24982. The Hotel Estrelícia also provides for riding excursions.

GOLF

Madeira only has one golf course, a 9-hole (5,244 yards)

course in Santo da Serra in the middle of the eastern part of the island, not far from the airport. Just a half-hour's drive from Funchal this course has all modern facilities, a club house and bar. Plans are moving ahead for the establishment of an 18-hole course in the near future.

HUNTING

For the hunting sportsman there are pigeon, partridge, quail and rabbit in season from October to December. Porto Santo is especially popular for this sport and the Tourist Board will have relevant details about hire of guns etc.

TENNIS

Most large hotels have tennis facilities which can sometimes be used by non-residents. In Caniço de Baixo the Reis Magos Tourism Complex has a number of courts. Tennis equipment can be purchased at several sports shops in Funchal.

SWIMMING

Many hotels have their own swimming pools, either on the coastal level or on the hotel roof. At the Lido Complex out to the west of Funchal the Olympic size pool and large pool for children provide ample facilities for those not able to get to a pool or swimming cove on the island like those at Porto Moniz. Open from 8 a.m. until 7 p.m. in summer and from 9 a.m. until 6 p.m. in winter the complex is also a centre for Madeira's water sports. As there are no beaches on Madeira in the resort sense, some big rock pools provide the opportunity for sea bathing but the popular Lido attracts most visitors whose hotel has no pool. Visitors looking for a long sandy beach will have to travel to Porto Santo. One of the island's biggest attractions is its beautiful sandy strand which stretches for almost 5 miles (8 kms.).

SEA SPORTS

Water sports are a big attraction on Madeira and the yachtsman or sailor will find an excellent marina for more than one hundred craft at Funchal. From the Clube Naval do Funchal, Amigos do Mar, Rota do Atlantico and several hotels, sailing boats can be rented. Contact the Tourist Board for details of organised boat excursions to Ponta do Sol in the west, Caniçal to the east, or the Ilhas Desertas one day's trip to the south. Ferries take visitors to Porto Santo, also a round trip of a full day. Motor boats can also be hired in Funchal port. Most of the larger hotels offer windsurfing equipment and waterskiing facilities and can organise custom-built water activities. Scuba diving and snorkelling are popular on Madeira because of the underwater caves which surround the island and the varied marine life in this sub-tropical sea. The Desert Isles, to the south of Madeira are also popular for underwater exploration. Contact the Inter Atlas Hotel at Garajau-Caniço for details. Tel: 932421.

FISHING

Deep sea fishing is very popular and specially equipped excursions can be joined for some hotels, like the Dom Pedro, or the Madeira Game Fishing Centre can help with information about fishing trips. Also contact Amigos do Mar et Calçado Cabo Queira on Tel: 23941. Once out in the ocean, swordfish (espadarte), spearfish, amberjack, blue marlin, blue hammerhead, porbeagle and thresher shark, bluefin, bigeye and longtail tuna (atum), are there for the taking in the great expanse of the Atlantic. Anglers will note that several international fishing records have been broken in the waters around Madeira. Other fish, like turbot

Deep sea tuna fishing

(*cherne*), cod (*bacalhau* – the national fish), sea eel (*eirós*), skate (*raia*), sea bass (*robalo*) and the famous, yet ugly, black scabbard fish (*peixe-espada*) which is taken from a depth of around 6,000 ft (2,000 m.) and are usually left to the professional island fishermen. Many enthusiasts fish from the craggy shoreline as the water is very deep immediately offshore. Trout (*truta*) fishing is done in the island's many streams and waterways and these fish are also farmed in certain areas to stock the fishing locations.

LOCAL DIVERSIONS

Apart from the attractions of sporting activities, sightseeing and just relaxing, Madeira offers numerous entertainment opportunities apart from the facilities available in the larger hotels. Bars, snack bars, cafés and restaurants present varied settings including the marina-style yacht restaurant *Vagrant*, the unusual 'Bar on the Rocks', or 'By the Sea', a seafood restaurant built into a natural sea cavern. Listen to the moving strains of the local 'fado' singers in Marcelino's Bar or dance at Vespas Discothèque – discothèques are known locally as 'boites'. Gamblers can try their luck at Funchal's only casino on Rua da Pontinha, the Casino da Madeira.

More relaxing than the tense pastime of roulette or chemin-de-fer is the local custom of rounding off the day with a chat on Madeira's terraces or outside its little cafés. With magnificent views from almost any point on the island it is enough for some visitors to just stroll through the island's villages and select a bar or café for refreshments with the friendly locals.

TOURING ON MADEIRA

The main island of Madeira is rugged and mountainous and there are few places where the terrain is flat. This means that the roads are tortuous and often steep. Car hire, taxis, the local bus services and coach tours are the best way to get around the island for long distances. However the most popular pastime and certainly the best way of enjoying Madeira's unrivalled countryside, is to take to the numerous footpaths and tracks which form a network across the island.

BY FOOT

The ideal way to tour in Madeira is to take transport to a pre-destined point on the island and then cut off into the interior on foot, following one or another of the popular walks. These paths often follow the *levadas*, or irrigation channels which bring water in decreasing levels from the mountain heights. Many of these *levada* walks are not for the inexperienced as some take courses around precipices and cliff edges, tunnelling through mountains and plunging into steep-sided gorges. Sensible walking shoes are a must, as is the right clothing for this rough terrain and the varying weather which can produce thick mists in the highlands and bright sunshine in the valleys. Waterproof clothing is recommended as is sufficient food and water for the intended walk. Remember that there is a very short twilight on this island because of its latitude and don't forget that, if you have left your transport in one particular spot, the only way of getting back to it may be completing a round trip. Making the return journey can often take longer than the outward hike.

A map, or guide is essential, and one must be prepared for the time it takes to complete a selected walk and the energy needed for some of the more strenuous walks. The Tourist Office is most helpful in providing information about the walks on Madeira and there are detailed books available for the keen walker who wishes to explore the island. One particularly useful book which describes a number of tours, walking trips from the gentle strolls to the rugged hikes, is

'Path in the Clouds' Pico Ruivo

entitled *Landscapes of Madeira*. This helpful guide gives details of transport, advice to walkers, places to visit on the walks, picnic locations, beauty spots and refreshment stops along the way. Several excellent, detailed maps are included in this guide which is an essential addition to the backpack of anyone with the desire to explore the highways and byways of Madeira's magnificent countryside.

BY CAR

A taxi or hire car gives visitors the freedom of the island but, if you are driving, remember to keep to the right, watch out for unexpected rock slides, potholes, moving or stationary obstacles around bends and often breathtakingly sheer-sided roads hugging steep precipices. Wearing a seat belt is obligatory and the speed limit is 60 k.p.h. in built-up areas and 90 k.p.h. elsewhere. However, as Madeira's roads are so winding and steep, the average speed is generally no more than around 20 k.p.h. When driving to a particular spot in order to make an excursion into the countryside by foot, park well off the road and let someone know which route you intend taking.

There are about four popular drives which enable the visitors to get a good impression of the island's landscape without walking any great distance. These routes give one a taste for the island and encourage anyone who is unfamiliar with the island to be more ambitious and attempt some of the established walks with confidence. On Madeira's coastal route, there are lookouts, belvederes and viewpoints around almost every bend. Don't, however, expect to cover any great distance in a day's outing as there are so many sights and distracting beauty spots that it is tempting to keep stopping the car.

There is one main road, Route 101, which completes a circuit of the entire island with detours to take in some of the more isolated points like the Ponta de São Lourenço peninsula and a few coastal villages. Four good roads cross the island widthwise, the longer and more difficult of which is that which runs from a point between Ponta do Sol and Madalena do Mar on the south coast, to the outskirts of Porto Moniz at the island's most north-westerly point. This road begins as the steep Route 208 and joins with the mountain crest road known as Route 204. The route crosses the western sector of the island diagonally along the 'backbone' ridge of mountains. The less steep and easiest road crossing of the island however, is located almost in the centre of Madeira and is known as Route 104. This road follows two great valleys which cut into the mountain ridge and almost link in the centre of the island. From the coastal road in the south, Route 104 runs from the town of Ribeira Brava, hugging the river's course and crossing the mountain range at Chão dos Louros, winding down into the Ribeira de São Vicente valley and meeting the north coast road at the town of São Vicente. Heading north out of Funchal, Route 103 runs up through the town of Monte, across the mountain peaks at Poiso and down through the northern valley of two rivers, the Seca and Metade, to emerge on the north coast at Faial. The last of these cross-island roads, Route 102, heads north-east out of Funchal to the town of Camancha and on, past the hillside town of Santo de Serra to link with Route 101 at Portela.

Each of these roads traverse a different part of Madeira's varied landscape and offer the traveller numerous viewpoints, beauty spots and picnic areas along the way. The more important of these stop-offs are given along each route and full descriptions of towns and villages and major points of interest can be found in the Gazetteer. Each route is taken separately and several detours are indicated to include nearby belvederes, or important sites. The main roads are prefixed (EN) but only the Route numbers are used hereon.

ROUTE 101

Madeira's peripheral road is best divided into two sections – the journey from Funchal in the south, (initially taking Route 215 and then Route 214) around the coast to Porto Moniz in the extreme north-west of the island, and then the road from Porto Moniz, along the north coast route, back to the capital. Several tunnels are passed through on this route and there are points where the road turns to trackway (on the detours) and others where the cliffside road is quite precarious.

FUNCHAL – PORTO MONIZ

FUNCHAL – CÂMARA DE LOBOS – CABO GIRÃO – RIBEIRA BRAVA – CALHETA – PONTA DO PARGO – PORTO MONIZ

[About 4 hours driving]

Heading west out of Funchal, past the Pontinha, keeping to the coastal road and passing Reid's Hotel on the left, the Avenido do Infante turns into the Estrada Monumental which runs due west past numerous aparthotels and resort areas including the Lido Swimming Pool complex to the left. Now on Route 215, past Ponta da Cruz, the road turns inland at Câmera de Lobos and there is one fine view back to the village a short distance up into the hills at Torre. Continue on the 214 to link with Route 101 at Estreito de Câmara de Lobos. A few minutes further on, over the bridge across the Ribeiro da Caldeira, a road to the left leads down to the famous Cabo Girão cliff and a spectacular belvedere. Take the detour to the belvedere but return to the main road and cross the Ribeira da Quinta Grande and the Quinta will be on the left.

The next good viewpoint is a lot further on, just before entering the town of Ribeira Brava. This is where an alternative road, Route 104, leads off to the right, across the island to São Vicente on the north coast. Avoid continuing on Route 101, and divert to the straighter, coastal road, the 213. This road runs through Ponta do Sol (two series of tunnels) and links with Route 101 again at Madalena do

Mar, however, the winding 101 should be avoided in preference to Route 213. Here there is another stop-over point favoured by most travellers for its magnificent views and the provision of a specially designated picnic area and a belvedere. From here it is only a track which continues for a short distance to meet with the better surfaced section of Route 213 and this is the route which should be taken, through the town of Calheta linking briefly with Route 101 at the Estreito da Calheta, where it changes into Route 212.

In order to avoid the winding Route 101, the road can be taken through Jardim do Mar and Paúl do Mar. This route, the 212 again, does not, however give the best viewpoints as these are located at turnings off the 101 at Prazeres, where the road goes down to a lookout over the coast, and another, a little further on, after crossing the Levada called Ponta do Pargo, or the Levada Calheta. Route 212 is semi-surfaced but there is another stunning viewpoint on this road, near the tunnel, just before it heads up to join with Route 101. Now the road has almost reached the furthest point west on Madeira and, after another series of twists and turns a track due west from the main highway leads out to the lookout at Ponta do Pargo. A good deal further on along Route 101, heading north but winding like a demented snake, the sign for the Santa pensão (pension) is passed on the left and the road begins to descend to Porto Moniz. Two excellent lookouts are located on this tortuous short stretch of the road before entering the town itself.

PORTO MONIZ – FUNCHAL

PORTO MONIZ – RIBEIRA DA JANELA – SÃO VICENTE – PONTA DELGARDA – SÃO JORGE – SANTANA – FAIAL – PENA DE ÁGUIA – PORTELA – MACHICO – SANTA CRUZ – FUNCHAL

[About 6 hours driving]

Not a couple of minutes after leaving Porto Moniz the famous rocks of the Ribeira da Janela should be viewed and, after passing through a tunnel system and hugging the coast on a comparatively straight stretch of road, another tunnel has been provided with a spectacular belvedere. Pass Seixal,

Rustic manor in Queimadas de Santana

over the Ribeira do Seixal, to another lookout, also at a tunnel location, and, a few minutes further on, the pretty town of São Vicente is reached. Route 104 cuts back over the island to the south coast at Ribeira Brava from here, but the 101 should be followed out of São Vicente, through another tunnel series at Ponta Delgada, to a fantastic lookout situated overlooking the north coast cliffs.

Just after this lookout, the road cuts inland to another belvedere at Boaventura and then doubles back, through another tunnel, along a winding route, to a famous beauty spot and picnic area at Arco São Jorge on the coast. Continue along the north coast, through São Jorge and over the river of the same name to the delightful town and popular tourist attraction of Santana. After Santana there are three spectacular viewpoints on the road, the last being after Faial, at the Penha de Águia (Eagle) mountain. Just before Porto da Cruz, another lookout commands the coastline down to Ponta São Lourenço and, from here, the road turns south and inland.

Portela is the next stop-off and there is a belvedere and restaurant here. The road at Portela divides off into either Route 102, which heads back over the mountains, via Camacha, to Funchal, or Route 101 which continues south and east to Machico. This route should be followed along the valley with a steep escarpment to the right, down into the town of Machico. A detour could be made just before entering Machico, to the left, on Route 101–3. This road cuts out due north and west, through a lengthy tunnel, along the famous peninsula of the Ponta de São Lourenço. At the very end of this fascinating drive is a fantastic lookout at the Ponta do Buraco, facing south, and another, on the north side of the narrow spit of rock, overlooking Pedra Furada.

Back on Route 101 at Machico, there is a popular lookout and picnic areas around Água de Pena, overlooking the Ponta da Queimada. Past the airport, at Santa Cruz, there is a picnic area and another long tunnel and then little of real significance before the road enters Caniço. Diversions to the many headlands around here are signposted but the famous lookout is that at Ponta do Garajau, just after Caniço town. One last belvedere before reaching Funchal again, is that just outside the city at Pináculo.

ROUTE 208/204 ARCO DA CALHETA - PORTO MONIZ

ARCO DA CALHETA - CAMPO GRANDE - LAVADA DO PAÚL - PAÚL DA SERRA - RABAÇAL - FONTE DO BISPO - LEVADA GRANDE - PORTO MONIZ

[About 2 hours driving]

On the south coast part of Route 101, at a point above Madalena do Mar, and in the area of the Arco da Calheta, Route 208 cuts up, away from the coast, into the high mountains in the west of Madeira. This is a tough route and quite precipitous in places, with spectacular scenic mountain and plateau views. As the road winds up steeply and nears the top of the high plateau a picnic spot has been established. After Campo Grande, a flat, high, table-top region, which the road skirts around, on the very top of the plateau overlooking the Paúl da Serra mountains, the road branches four ways. To the immediate right is a road, the 204, for Encumeada, in the saddle of the central mountain range; the next right is a route to São Vicente on the north coast, the 208; another route, the 209, is not well surfaced and leads directly down to Porto Moniz on the north-east coast; and the route selected, the turning to the left, Route 204, takes the visitor across the mountain ridgetop, also to Porto Moniz.

This continuation of Route 204, crosses the Lavada do Paúl where there is a fine viewpoint over the Paúl da Serra. A detour to the right leads to an excellent picnic spot at Rabaçal. After this junction the road runs straight and heads due west for a time until the spectacular beauty spot, lookout and picnic area at Fonte do Bispo. Continuing down towards the coast, before leaving the high ridge of the plateau, a belvedere is located at Quebradas. From here Route 204 heads north to meet with Route 101 on the easternmost coast after crossing the Levada Grande. Turn right at this junction and, within a few minutes the town of Porto Moniz is in sight.

ROUTE 104   RIBEIRA BRAVA - SÃO VICENTE

RIBEIRA BRAVA – SERRA DE ÁGUA – VINHÁTICOS – ENCUMEADA – CHAO DOS LOUROS – ROSÁRIO – RIBEIRA DE SÃO VICENTE – SÃO VICENTE

[About a one hour drive]

Again from the south coastal section of Route 101, at the town of Ribeira Brava, the island-crossing Route 104, heads due north, following the course of the River Brava valley on a long, straight road to Serra de Água. It is just after Serra de Água that one comes to the first real lookout on this route. In the area around Vinháticos and its Pousada, there are several very popular picnic sites and an excellent belvedere looking right down the valley and around to the steep mountains on each side. From Vinháticos the road winds up towards the saddle of the mountain range which runs the length of the island. Halfway up to the highest point, Route 216, heading up into the mountains and running due east, is on the right. However, continue up to the top and it is here, at the Chão dos Louros, that there are several magnificent viewpoints. Picnic areas have also been located on this, the highest point on Route 104. This is the region of Encumeada and Route 204, across the western plateau is on the left. From Encumeada it is possible to make a short walking detour to see the picturesque Levada do Norte. After Chão dos Louros, the road winds down the mountainside towards the valley of the Ribeira de São Vicente and continues, along that valley, past Rosário and Feiteiras, where the Nossa Sẽnhora da Fâtima clock tower stands out on the hillside, and then down to the town of São Vicente itself.

ROUTE 103   FUNCHAL – FAIAL

FUNCHAL – MONTE – CURRAL DOS ROMEIROS – POISO – BALCÕES – RIBEIRO FRIO – SÃO ROQUE DO FAIAL – PENHA DE ÁGUIA

[About one hour's driving]

This island-crossing road has numerous detours to picnic spots and popular viewpoints and beauty spots. Heading out of Funchal, north, along the Rua 31 de Janeiro, keeping the cutting of the Santa Luzia river to the left, turn right to the Quinta do Til along the Rua do Til, heading for Monte. It is worth taking a break here to walk around this interesting little town with its Baroque style church and Quinta. After the town of Monte there is a popular belvedere to the right, overlooking the Curral dos Romeiros, but this is a detour

Pico Arieiro

through the town itself. The road, however, doubles back before entering the town and heads up to the famous viewpoint at Terreiro da Luta. Again this belvedere is on a side track from the main 103 route, as it lies to the right of Route 201, just after it meets with the 103. Back on the north-bound Route 103, the village of Poiso is passed where Route 202 crosses the road. It is possible to take a short detour on the left to Pico Arieiro. From here a path leads to Pico Ruivo and, just over the ridge to the south-west, in the valley of the Ribeira do Curral, is the famous Curral das Freiras which is best reached on a separate road from Funchal, the 107. Just after Poiso, on the right, are a couple of well-loved picnic spots. The great peaks of the Eira do Serrado and those of Pico do Arieiro and Pico Ruivo dominate the skyline to the west from the road to Ribeiro Frio. More picnic areas have been built around the Ribeiro Frio area on the edge of the plateau scarp just a short distance further north from Poiso where the road crosses the Levada do Furado. To the left is the famous lookout of the Balcões (the balconies) and, a little further down the hillside road, on the left, there is another popular belvedere and several picnic sites. The road now doubles back on itself and cuts down into the valley of the Ribeira da Metade which shares its wide valley floor with the Ribeira Seca. Running between the twin rivers, Route 103 cuts a straight, level pathway through pastures, to meet with the north coastal Route 101 at the famous site of the Penha de Águia, or Eagle Rock, seen on the right-hand side of the road. Faial is now just a short drive down to the river valley and most visitors who take this route will want to go on to the picturesque region of Santana, one of Madeira's major attractions just a few minutes on the road to the west.

ROUTE 102   FUNCHAL - PORTELA

FUNCHAL - LEVADA DOS TORNOS - VALÉ DO PARAÍSO - CAMANCHA - ÁGUAS MANSAS - QUATRO ESTRADAS - LEVADA DO PORTELA - PORTELA

[About one hour's driving]

Take the Rua João de Deus road west out of the capital,

The view from Machico cliffs

crossing both the Santa Luzia and João Gomes river channels and then follow the Dr Manuel Pestana Junior route on the left immediately after the Gomes gulley. This road cuts across to the start of Route 102. The tortuous road winds past the Quinta do Pomar before crossing the Levada dos Tornos, linking with Route 102 coming in from the right before crossing the levada again. There is a famous lookout just off the road to the right before the second levada crossing. The Quinta Palheiro Ferreiro is also on the right of the road. Winding again, the road runs past the Valé do Paraíso (Paradise Valley) on the left and comes down into the town of Camacha. More twists and turns after Camacha, past the tiny settlement of Eira de Fora leads to a crossing over the Levada do Pico at Águas Mansas. Here the road is joined on the right by Route 206. Quatro Estradas, a little further on is a favourite stopping point and from here the road is rather straight but with marvellous views across the Boaventura Valley, to its junction with Route 207 coming in from the right. Some visitors take the opportunity to divert off to the lovely village of Santo da Serra here. A wooded and hilly stretch of road is then followed until it passes over the tunnel of the Levada do Portela and then into the town of Portela itself where there is a fine lookout and restaurant. From Portela it is only a few minutes drive down into the island's second most important town, Machico.

These five main routes are just some examples of the many roads and tracks which can be selected from a good map of

Madeira like the Michelin maps or those supplied locally. Combinations of these routes can be selected for a round trip from Funchal back to Funchal for example. Details of the places and sights mentioned in the preceding tours and many other points of interest are provided in the Gazetteer pages 105–120. Funchal and its immediate environs, with recommended tours, are described in the following chapter.

FUNCHAL

BACKGROUND

It was Prince Henry the Navigator who decided that Madeira's discoverer, João Zarco, should have governorship of that part of the island which now includes Funchal. In 1420 the prince divided the islands of Madeira and Porto Santo into three 'captaincies'. Drawing an imaginary line from Ponta da Oliveira, east of Funchal, diagonally across the island to Ponta do Tristão, the Portuguese ruler allocated the southern portion to Zarco and the northern part to Tristão Vaz Teixeira, the co-discoverer. A favourite of the realm, Bartolomeu Perestrello, was given jurisdiction over the island of Porto Santo.

It was inevitable that Funchal would be chosen as the island's main port and capital as it lay in the lee of towering mountains, at a point where three rivers met in one large estuary, and, politically, it was located in Zarco's part of the island. A natural amphitheatre surrounded its deep harbour and the city's south-facing aspect protected it from the prevailing north-east winds. All these facts made Funchal a perfect choice for the site of an important port. From the sea, the beautiful, greenery-clad bay of Funchal must have seemed an ideal spot for Zarco to make his home. Landing on the rocky shoreline in 1420, the early explorers could not

Funchal from the east

help noticing the abundant fennel which grew in clumps among the laurel bushes and conifer trees. The liquorice scent of these wild herbs in the salty, ocean breeze must have been exquisite, so much so that they named the spot Funchal after the prolific plant.

Although Funchal was not the spot where Zarco and his crew had first landed on discovering Madeira – that location lay in the area given to Teixeiro – the Portuguese captain had selected the ideal place in which to settle. Within weeks he had planned his future city and had begun allocating pieces of land to would-be colonists. It was a shame that one of these settlers was over-zealous in clearing his plot of land. Thick woods and bracken, tangled bushes and furze covered the steep hillside and the task of clearing the dense undergrowth by hand seemed too much toil to one eager settler. Setting fire to the heather, the poor chap never realised that, not only would he be clearing his own plot of land, but he would be responsible for clearing the entire island! Fanned by the ocean winds, the fire on Madeira burned for many years – some say seven. Eventually the hapless arsonist returned to his blackened plot of land and Zarco's plan for the island's first town began to rise from the ashes.

A knight at the Court of Prince Henry, Zarco was able to send for his family as soon as the first houses had been built on the hillside surrounding Funchal's half-moon bay. As was the tradition when settling a newly-discovered land, he initially set about constructing a church. Facing the rolling surf of Funchal harbour, the Chapel of Santa Catarina was erected in 1425 and is now the oldest remaining building on Madeira. This little chapel is open to the public and this is where our first tour of Funchal's interesting sites begins.

Five-and-a-half centuries of history has produced, in Funchal, an interesting and varied city with pretty streets; cobbled, narrow alleyways; wide, flowered boulevards; palm-lined avenues and historic squares. Today, attractive white-painted houses with red-tiled roofs stand next to yellowing, traditionally grandiose structures. Churches and monasteries faced with ancient dark volcanic stone contrast with whitewashed walls and bright-shuttered windows. On the hillside slopes the houses' colourful doors and awnings emulate the reds, blues and greens of the flowering plants which pervade every nook and cranny.

TOURING FUNCHAL

Funchal's long esplanade gives the city a frontage which makes it easier for visitors who can use this promenade to orientate walking excursions through the city. Running the length of the harbour, the sea wall curves from east to west and it is at the westerly end of the city that the first tour of Funchal begins. It is convenient to divide the area of Funchal and its surrounds into four sectors of easily manageable tours.

- The West Central tour, beginning from the Chapel of Santa Catarina, overlooking the harbour and taking in some of the more historic sites, returning to Parque Santa Catarina.

- The Central tour, beginning at the Fortaleza de São Lourenço near the Santa Catarina Chapel and ending in the city's central square.

- The East-Central tour starting from just north of the city square, at the Law Courts, and terminating at the Fortaleza de São Tiago, at the eastern end of the waterfront promenade.

- The Outskirts tour, a selection of points of interest around the city best visited by taxi, car or bus.

WEST-CENTRAL TOUR

[Allow half a day to complete in comfort]

Parque de Santa Catarina

This tour begins in the Parque de Santa Catarina, named after Zarco's chapel, Madeira's oldest building. Constructed in 1425, the white-painted chapel of Santa Catarina is located just west of the bridge over the São João River and is open to the public. It is set in the grounds of the park which was once an ancient graveyard, the Cemiterio das Augustas. The statue of Christopher Columbus in the decorative gardens of the park was erected in 1968 to commemorate the great explorer's short stay in Funchal. There are two Quintas, or country mansions, around Santa Catarina Park. Look for the Quinta das Augustas which is only open to the public on request, and the Quinta Vigia, now the city casino, but once the residence of the Empress Elizabeth of Austria. This is situated to the west of the park and the casino was built here by the designer of Brasilia City, Oscar Niemeyer, in 1979.

Church of Santa Clara

By the time Zarco was in his mid-fifties he resolved to build another church as a suitable location for his family's tombs. He therefore established the Church of Santa Clara in about 1450, high up on the hillside above the Chapel of Santa Catarina. This is the next historic monument on this short tour. From the Chapel and the Parque Santa Catarina this church is reached by crossing Avenida do Infante, past the monument to the Infante Don Henrique at the Praca do Infante. On the left-hand side, on the north side of Avenida do Infanta, is the Dona Amelia Hospital with its famous botanical gardens guarded at the entrance by two large dragon trees. From Santa Catarina Park it is best to take some form of transport up to the historic Church of Santa Clara as it is a steep walk.

One of Funchal's most historic buildings, the Convent of Santa Clara is situated in the north-west part of the city, on the Calcada de Santa Clara, and is open to the public. The present Santa Clara church was reconstructed in the seventeenth century on the site of Zarco's original structure and his grand, canopied tomb, supported by classical lions and embellished with traditional carved tracery lies in a niche in the church. The highly-decorative tiling which clads the church's walls is known as *azulejos* and is typical of the decoration of Portuguese buildings built between the sixteenth and eighteenth centuries. After Zarco's death, in 1467, his two granddaughters established a convent (the Order of St Clare) adjacent to the church. This has a fine cloistered quadrangle enhanced by orange trees, where the tombs of Zarco's granddaughters are to be found. Look also for the ancient crucifix which dates back to the reconstruction of the convent.

Quinta das Cruzes

Just a short walk north of the convent, is the villa of Quinta das Cruzes on the steep Calcada do Pico. This lavishly-decorated mansion was once the residency of Zarco and stands in equally luxurious botanical gardens. Sensibly occupying the upper floor of the villa, Zarco must have had magnificent views over his city and its neat little harbour. Around 1452, sugar cane began to be grown on the island and this brought immense prosperity to the island. This wealth can now be seen in the structure and lavish interior of the Quinta which is now a museum containing many unique examples of decorative art. These include seventeenth-century Chinese porcelain, eighteenth-century enamels from France, old English silver, East India Company china, exquisite paintings and a marvellous collection of ivories. Antique Portuguese and English furniture fill the rooms. Note that some of the Brazilian rosewood and mahogany pieces were constructed from wooden crates which were used to transport the island's precious sugar. This furniture was known locally as *caixa de açúcar*, or sugar-box furniture. A large collection of architectural antiques are displayed in the Quinta's gardens and its Orchid House is a particular attraction.

After Zarco's death Funchal continued to prosper – especially from its trade in sugar. The town had its own coat of arms which depicts five sugar loaves as testament to the riches derived from this crop, initially brought from Italy. A famous visitor to the city in 1479, also of Italian origin, was Christopher Columbus, who resided here at the home of João Esmeraldo. Columbus had just married Beatriz Moniz, daughter of the governor of nearby Porto Santo, and they

View of Funchal's harbour and western headland

honeymooned in Funchal for a short time. Funchal was, by then growing into a sizeable town and several of the original buildings of the fifteenth century can be seen on the walk from the Quinta das Cruzes.

Forte de São João do Pico

Of particular interest is the next point of call in the tour. Still in the north-west sector of Funchal and continuing up the Calcada do Pico is the Forte de São João do Pico, on Rua do Castelo. The 'Fort of St John of the Peak' was built in 1632 and is only open to the public on request, which can be got from the Tourist Board, but the view over Funchal from here is stupendous. Forte do Pico (das Frias) is just one of the city's three major fortresses. Originally the old town lay between the protective forts of São Lourenço, down on the Avenido do Mar esplanade, and the Forte de São Tiago to the east of the waterfront.

Church of Saint Peter

Retracing one's steps down the Calcada de Santa Clara, past the Quinta das Cruzes and the Convento Santa Clara on the right, at the crossroads with Rua São Pedro, are two important sights. On the left is the Church of St Peter, an historic monument and open to the public.

The Municipal Museum – Palacio do São Pedro

Opposite is the Municipal Museum, sometimes referred to as the Palacio do São Pedro. This was once the residence of Count Carvalhal. Open every day, (Mon–Sat 9.30-5, Sunday 12-5)the museum contains natural history exhibits, an aquarium and a variety of stuffed marine species, birds and animals in the upstairs gallery.

Jardim de São Fransisco

Continuing on down towards the harbour the road turns into a narrow flight of steps leading to Rua Ivens and the large Jardim de São Fransisco. This beautiful park contains ornate gardens, exotic trees and an ornamental pond.

Teatro Municipal

Cross the park to the south-east corner and the Teatro Municipal is directly ahead across the Boulevard of Avenida Arriaga. This still functional theatre is an historic building and has recently been refurbished. Keeping on the São

Francisco Park side of the tree-lined boulevard and walking east, the Tourist Information Centre is located in the next block, as is the main Post Office.

The Old Wine Lodge – The Armazem

Next to the Tourist Office is the Armazem, or Old Wine Lodge. Operated by a number of wine producers, the visitor can taste the various selections of Madeira wine and also buy samples from its shop. An audio-visual show demontrates the methods used in wines production and there is a museum inside the Lodge, or cellars.

The St Lawrence Fortress – Palacio de São Lourenço

Across from the Tourist Board is the São Lourenço. The St Lawrence Fortress is now a Portuguese National Monument and was constructed in the sixteenth century. This was the first fort built on Madeira. The impressive edifice is now a military base and not open to the public but its unusual design with cannon, shuttered windows and ornate battlements makes a good backdrop for tourist photos. Across the Avenida do Mar is the pleasantly shaded and flower-bordered Avenida das Comunidades Madeirenses which extends from the outlet of the São João river to the outflows of both the Santa Luzia and João Gomez rivers. The beach here is of smooth shingles. It is worth a short detour to walk out onto the small jetty which extends out into the harbour in the shadow of the fort as one can view the city in perspective from the tip of the landing stage. The little road down the west side of Fortaleza de São Lourenço continues on to emerge by the Parque Santa Catarina where this short tour of north-west Funchal began. This mini-circuit of the major sites of west-central Funchal, could take a half-day to complete comfortably.

CENTRAL TOUR

[Allow a good half-day for this excursion]

This is a tour that might include one of the modes of transport peculiar to Madeira, the *carros de bois*, or ox-drawn sledge. On the Avenida das Comunidades Madeirenses these curious wagons, rather like small, wickerwork four-poster beds on runners, are towed across Funchal's smooth-cobbled streets by pairs of bullocks, yoked together and steered by traditionally-dressed operators. In the old days this method of transport was used to ferry wine barrels and other goods around the city. Today the boater-hatted carters still dress in white uniform but the *carros* have been converted to take visitors on sedate tours around the city sights. However, it is probably easier to see more of the historic monuments and their interiors by taking a short walking tour.

The St Lawrence Fortress – Palacio de São Lourenço
A tour of central Funchal could begin at the Forteleza de São Lourenço as it is conveniently situated in the middle of the waterfront boulevard. From the fort, following the Avenida do Mar eastwards, past one block, the Museu de Alfandega is on the left, facing the port.

The Customs House – Museu de Alfandega
This is the city's ancient Customs House, also a national monument. A classical building, the Customs House was constructed in the sixteenth century during the reign of Manuel I. Rua da Alfandega, running along the north flank of this historic building is worth seeing for its unusual, black lava paving stones and the ancient buildings which line the narrow street. Walking north, and keeping this quaint little alleyway to the right, across another road junction, the Cathedral Square lies up ahead.

Cathedral Sé
The Cathedral Sé, built in the late fifteenth century, between 1485 and 1515, during the time of King Manuel I, by the Knights of the Order of The Cross, was the first Portuguese cathedral to be built outside the mainland. The name Sé refers to the Holy See. The cathedral's imposing frontage is set off by its square, black basalt and white-washed stone belfry and clock tower, its patterned, *azulejos* tiled spire and cornet-like finials. Inside the cathedral is a masterpiece of early Portuguese artistry with a Moorish-style, ivory-inlaid cedar and juniper wood ceiling and delicately-painted tracery arches. A pageant of religious statues stand in highly-decorated oaken niches around the choir stalls which face into the apse which focuses on the sixteenth-century high altar piece, a Flemish painting

The graceful interior of Cathedral Sé

commemorating Our Lady of Fatima. The Cathedral of Sé's artistry depicts the exotic discoveries of the time, curious animals, trees and flowers represented in the carvings relate to the many tropical species found in the Indies, the Caribbean and South America during the times of early exploration. A marble pulpit and font complete the serene, but ornate interior which comfortably combines several architectural and artistic styles. In the Treasury there is a silver-gilt crucifix donated by King Manuel I.

Plaza of Sé Cathedral
The Plaza of Sé Cathedral is at the end of the Avenida Arriaga and, from its brickwork and whitewashed frontage, looking down the boulevard, the large building on the right is the Palacio do Governo Regional, or Local Governor's Palace. Look for the fine bronze statue of the city's founder, João Gonçalves Zarco. Also note the grandiose surrounding buildings like the bank. Back at the cathedral frontage, face north and take the narrow Rua João Tavira up towards its junction with Rua da Carriera, the location of the famous statue of 'The Sower'.

The Praca do Municipio

Turn immediately right at the junction and one is almost in the city's main plaza, the Praca do Municipio. There are four major sights of interest around Funchal's main square and probably the main attraction is the Museu de Arte Sacra, Museum of Sacred Art, situated on Rua do Bispo, or Bishop's Street.

Museum of Sacred Art – Museu de Arte Sacra

Walk just around the right corner of the square into the narrow street and the one-time Bishop's Palace fronts onto the road. One of the most spectacular collections of Flemish religious art is housed in this seven-galleried museum. Religious treasures and artifacts, some dating from the sixteenth century are on display as are fifteenth- and sixteenth-century Portuguese and Flemish paintings. This rich collection of religious works of art has been amassed from ancient churches all over the island. Flemish painters who worked in Madeira, traders from Antwerp and merchants from Bruges, all contributed to the wealth of sacred art now displayed in the museum – and all were attracted to the island by its sugar. Sugar was exchanged for Flemish artworks, bartered for sacred icons and given in exchange for artists' skills. Over four hundred years of art treasures now fill the austere building.

Church of St John the Evangelist – Igréja do Colégio

Back in the Municipal Square, the imposing façade to the

Praca do Municipio in Funchal's main square

north of the chequer-paved plaza is the Jesuit-style Church of St John the Evangelist, the former College, or Igréja do Colégio. Heavy basalt stone surrounds outline the porticos, windows and the four niches containing statues of saints, sharply contrasting with the whitewashed exterior. On the third level Saints Ignatius and Francis Xavier look down on the square and, each side of the three doorways, Saints Francis Borgia and Stanisias gaze out towards the central memorial with its fountains. Inside this impressive building with its adjacent, red-tiled monastery, a baroque nave is decorated with the ubiquitous *azulejos* tiles with exotic, floral designs. The candelabra and altar furnishings are exuberant examples of baroque art as is the painted ceiling. This seventeenth-century monument is open to the public, but the monastery next door is now a military barracks.

Town Hall – Funchal Câmara Município
To the east of the square is the Funchal Câmara Município, or Town Hall which is notable for its exquisite patio. The Town Hall was once an eighteenth-century palace, another residence of the Count of Carvalhal, and is only open to the public upon request. Just up the road to the left of the Town Hall are the City's Law Courts. This little tour from the Fortelza de São Lourenço up to the city square completes a good half-day's excursion, especially with the many distractions of other early buildings, pretty squares and narrow, cobbled streets.

EAST-CENTRAL TOUR

[Allow about, two hours for this tour]

Across the culvert-like gorge of the River Santa Luzia, to the east of the city centre, a short tour from the top of the city to the waterfront can take in at least seven historic monuments and places of interest. Crossing the river from Rua 5 de Outubro, behind the Law Courts, Rua P. Novas brings the walker out into the steep Calcada do Santa Luzia.

The Church of the Incarnation
Facing the bridge is the Church of the Incarnation. Entered through a little side door, this elegantly designed church dates to the late sixteenth century.

The Church of Santa Luzia

The Church of Santa Luzia stands off the Rua 31 de Janeiro and, following this road down the side of the river gully, the Church of Bom Jesus is located just to the left on the street of the same name. Continuing on down to the large junction where five main roads meet, the Church of Carmo lies up on the left. It is probably best to cut across the busy junction to the little street called Rua Dr F. Ornelas. At the bottom of this little street another river culvert is crossed. This is the River João Gomes which cuts down to the harbour from the north-east of Funchal city. As the river is crossed, directly in front is the market place.

The Market – Mercado dos Lavradores

The Mercado dos Lavradores, or 'market of the farmers', is open every day except Sundays, and encapsulates both the rural and suburban atmospheres of Madeira. A visit to the market should not be missed for its variety of produce, cross-section of people from town and villages across the island and its genuine ambiance of *bonhomie*. The modern building has a large central courtyard with a main hall. At the entrance flower sellers arrange their wares, dressed in the traditional costume of the island – trimmed red cape and hood, black tasselled cap known as a *carapucha*, blouse, candy-striped full skirt and loose leather boots called *botacha* – as is both the custom and the law of the land. Bird of Paradise flowers, Flamingo flowers, antirrhinums and orchids are just a few of the blooms which make up the flower-sellers' displays. Inside the market wickerwork baskets and trays overflow with fruits of all varieties both well known, like oranges, lemons and bananas, and more exotic species like annon, custard apple, mangoes, guavas and passion fruit. Vegetables of all kinds spill out across rush mats and the mosaic cobbles of the square and, in a hall next to the main market, one will find the fish stalls where the evil-looking scabbard fish can be seen on sale together with tunny, swordfish, tuna, bass and sardine.

Just a little way further down towards the quayside is the Fisherman's Quarter of the city where the main fish market is located and where there are many seafood restaurants along the narrow, cobbled lanes. Following the road running parallel to the seafront Avenida do Mar, to the east, Rua Don Carlos leads down to the Chapel of Espirito Santo and, just to the left of the Chapel is the Church of Santa Maria Maior.

Church of São Maria Maior

This eighteenth-century baroque church is strikingly white-washed between the great, black, carved basalt decorations which stand out in relief from the plain frontage. The ceiling of St Mary the Major is of interest as are the sacred relics on display. Thanksgivings for the miracles which saved Madeira from the plagues of 1523 and 1538, are performed outside this church every May Day. Just opposite the church is a lookout, called the Socorro, with views out over the bay, the harbour and to the Forteleza São Tiago, or Santiago Fort. This spectacular edifice is now part of the port complex and houses the coastguard's headquarters.

St James Fort

St James Fort, with its sombre, solid lava stone bulwarks and newer turrets, was originally constructed in 1614 and is named after St James the Less, the city's patron saint. Once the twin of the Forteleza de São Lourenço to the west of the city, guarding the port from marauding pirates and protecting the sugar galleons, the Forteleza de São Tiago (St James) now towers over fishing vessels and the warehousing loading docks of Funchal's inner harbour.

FUNCHAL'S OUTSKIRTS

There are some sights surrounding the capital's centre which are best visited by taking a taxi, bus or tour coach and, depending on where the visitor is based, these include the Quinta do Palheiro, east of Funchal, the Quinta da Palmeira and the Jardim Botanico to the north, and the Cais Molhe da Pontinha and Chapel of Nazareth in the west.

Quintas in Madeira were like grand country houses built amongst richly-manicured estates by wealthy merchants, retired officials of colonial times and by the Portuguese aristocracy. Often set in idyllic surroundings with stupendous views, several of these Quintas have been adapted into annexes, or embraced by the grounds of more recently-built hotels like the Quinta in the ten-acre grounds of Reid's Hotel west of the city. The more grandiose Quintas have been preserved as treasured examples of the opulent and relaxed life of Madeira enjoyed by the prosperous in past years.

Quinta do Palheiro

A good drive out of Funchal, to the north-east, the Quinta

do Palheiro is typical of Madeira's country estates. With 800 acres, including 30 acres of flower beds, the mansion belongs to one of the British families who made their home on the island many years ago. The Blandys are as much a part of Madeiran life as any of the mixed races which have settled in Madeira over the centuries. With interests in the Madeira wine business, in tourism and transport, the Quinta, often called the Palheiro Ferriero, or the 'Haystack Mansion of the Blacksmith', is one of the Blandy family's treasured possessions and a monument of intrinsic importance to the Madeiran heritage. Coach trips don't often visit this Quinta but tour operators can advise on transport and admission charges to the spectacular gardens.

Quinta da Palmeira

Another exquisite example of the Madeiran country estate is the Quinta da Palmeira, 'Palm Tree Mansion', to the north of Funchal. Paintings of the late seventeenth century show this mansion standing high on the mountains above the city of Funchal. Set on a steep escarpment at the end of a short path, this private residence is built on a terrace overlooking the capital. A Gothic-style window which forms a gazebo on the lawns is said to date from the late fifteenth century and some say it came from the house in which Christopher Columbus stayed during his residency with his friend, João Esmeraldo, in Funchal. To the west of Quinta da Palmeira, a short walk away is another country mansion, the Quinta do Til.

Quinta Bom Sucesso – Jardim Botanico – Botanical Gardens

East of the Quinta da Palmeira is the site of another ancient Quinta, the Bom Sucesso, 'Good Times Mansion'. In its grounds the Madeiran authorities have laid out the island's celebrated Jardim Botanico, or Botanical Gardens, designed on terraces looking down on the João Gomez river valley. From the top terrace the horseshoe bay of Funchal lies at your feet with the red tiles of villas and houses poking through lush island foliage as far as the eye can see. This is one of the most panoramic views of the city and a classic for the avid botanist or just the visitor who appreciates the wonders of nature which fills the expertly-tended gardens. Each example of tree, plant and flower has its Portuguese and Latin name inscribed in plaques and much of what has been achieved here has been due to the contributions of a Madeiran botanist, Carlos Azevedo de Menezes, after whom the wide entrance road has been named.

Cais Molhe da Pontinha
From the balcony at the Botanical Gardens there is an excellent view of the Cais Molhe da Pontinha, the great harbour arm, or the 'quay jetty of the moorings'. This should be included as one of Funchal's impressive sights and its entrance and control post is located at the far west end of the esplanade. It should be obvious why the wharf has this name as there are usually several cruise liners tied up along its 1,500 yard (1,350 m.) length. The Pontinha was originally much smaller when it was first constructed at the end of the eighteenth century and has been extended twice, only reaching its present length by 1962. The walk out along the wharf is well worth it for the panoramic view one gets of the city across the water.

Forteleza do Nossa Sěnhora de Conceicao
A little way along the jetty the road passes the Forteleza do Nossa Sěnhora de Conceicao (Our Lady of the Immaculate Conception), an ancient fort which is shown in maps and paintings of the seventeenth century. Once this fort stood on a rocky islet, reached only by boat and, together with the twin forts of São Lourenço and São Tiago, protected the harbour of Funchal and its shipping. At the very end of the Pontinha, permission should be requested to climb the sea wall for the wonderful view of Funchal and the far-off Ilhas Desertas to the south-west.

Chapel of Nazareth
Much further up in the hills to the north-west of Funchal, the Capela da Nazaré, or Chapel of Nazareth, is reached by passing the Pontinha on the left and taking the Pico dos Barcelos route. Down to the left, in the bay of the Seco river, just after the Pontinha, is a tiny islet, Ilha do Amor, the Isle of Love, reached by a narrow causeway. Join the Avenida Arriaga and turn off north, past the stadium, taking the Caminho da Nazaré turning from the Caminho das Virtudes. This isolated chapel was built in the seventeenth century. Note the early *azulejos* tiling on the chapel walls and the historic naval scene on one wall.

Lido Complex
If one continues along the coastal road, Estrada Monumental, there are a couple of Funchal's more modern attractions, the large Lido Complex with an Olympic-size pool, watersports centre and all the amenities of a holiday centre.

Funchal Naval Club
A little further along the coast is the Funchal Naval Club from where sailing excursions can be organised.

PORTO SANTO ISLAND

Shaped rather like a leaping game fish, this 8-mile (13 kms.) long, 4-mile (6 kms.) wide island is really a mini-archipelago. Eight tiny islets cluster round the main, comparatively flat and desert-like island. These include Ilhéu de Baixo ou da Cal, in the south and Ilhéu de Ferro to the west, (both of which form the 'fish's tail') and Ilhéu de Cima, forming the imaginary fish's beak in the east. Little islets along Porto Santo's northern coast give the 'fish' its dorsal fin. It is a happy coincidence that Porto Santo takes on the form of a fish, as fishing is one of this island's main industries. Just 16 square miles in area, the terrain of Porto Santo is quite different from that of mountainous Madeira, and much less attractive in terms of greenery. However, Porto Santo's lure is not only in its beaches, which extend along the island's 'underbelly', its magnetism lies in the wild, desert-like countryside, its relaxed atmosphere and placid people. The climate on Porto Santo is milder than Madeira's but its soil is like a rust-coloured chalk and therefore less fertile than its neighbouring island's rich loam.

No more than 5,000 people live on this plateau-like island which rises towards its highest peak, Pico do Facho (Beacon, or Torch Peak) at 1,676 ft. (511 m.) in the north of the island. Most of the inhabitants of Porto Santo live in the town of Porto Santo, also known as Vila Baleira. This little township is located on the island's south-east coast which is one long sandy beach – the only sandy beach in the Madeira group. Running 5½ miles (9 kms.) along the underside of this volcanic island, the beach attracts holidaymakers from the main island of Madeira 27 miles (40 kms.) away and also international visitors to the island group. Porto Santo town is the island's only port and, cutting across the centre of Porto Santo is the airport with a long runway built for NATO use. Aircraft flying out of Madeira used to refuel on Porto Santo as the Santa Catarina runway was not long enough to provide lift for a plane with a full passenger and fuel complement.

About one-and-a-half hour's sailing by hydrofoil from

A windmill on Porto Santo

Madeira and around 15 minutes flying time from Santa Catarina airport, Porto Santo is a haven of rest and relaxation. Only about 35 miles (55 kms.) of road and track criss-cross the island, but the main road links Porto Santo town with Ponta da Calheta in the far south, running along the edge of the long, golden beach. Porto Santo, 'Holy Port', was first discovered by accident when João Gonçlaves Zarco and Tristão Vaz Tiexeira were sent to explore the seas to the west of Africa by Henry the Navigator of Portugal. Shipwrecked on the island in 1418 the couple went on to discover Madeira the year after. In 1420 Bartholomeu Perestrello, a naturalised Portuguese, originally a Genoese, was given the governorship of the island, built the church and laid out the island's first settlement. Unwisely Perestrello introduced rabbits to the island which devastated any crops which the settlers tried to grow. Wisely, though, the first governor of Porto Santo agreed to let his daughter, Isabel Moniz, marry a travelling merchant who visited them whilst buying sugar in Funchal. His name was Christopher Columbus and the couple stayed for a while in the town of Porto Santo in 1479 before sailing to Funchal, Madeira. Isabel, after bearing a son, Diego, in the same year she married, died in Lisbon in 1484. Columbus, eight years later, sailed on to discover the Americas.

Successive attacks by pirates and seafarers forced the

island's inhabitants to retreat to the extinct volcano called Pico do Castelo (Castle Peak) until the Algerian and French marauders had finished sacking their town. Between pillages, droughts and famines, the islanders eventually established an agriculturally-based economy which now produces grapes, wheat, figs, melons, tomatoes and cereals. Porto Santo produces a sweet, white wine and the mineral water of Porto Santo is bottled and exported to Madeira. Locally-caught fish is canned on Porto Santo and the chalky soil provides the raw material for making lime and cement. Whereas on Madeira, the cattle are penned in to stop them straying over precipices, cattle graze freely on this flattish island and donkeys are used here as beasts of burden, unlike on rocky Madeira. Donkeys carrying their large wicker baskets and canvas-sailed windmills which grind the island's corn are typical sights in the arid country landscape.

VILA BALEIRA

Also known as Porto Santo, the island's only town has the impression of being more like a southern Spanish or even a Mexican town – exactly what one would expect in these warm latitudes. White-painted houses, bright green palms and pink and orange bougainvillea brighten what is a desert-type landscape reminiscent of Fuerteventura in the Canary Islands. Narrow, shady streets with whitewashed walls and a palm-lined boulevard leading up from the waterfront give this small port an almost Mediterranean atmosphere. The pretty little town of Porto Santo has a couple of thousand inhabitants and is located on the south-east side of the island, on a broad, sandy beach – the only real beach in the Madeiran archipelago. It was lucky for the discoverers, Zarco and Tiexeira, that Porto Santo had a 5½ mile-(9 kms.) long beach when he was caught in a storm off the island in 1418. If Zarco had been swept onto Porto Santo's neighbouring island, Madeira, the story of his shipwreck against that rocky coastline might never have been told – no wonder he named the place where he landed, Porto Santo, 'Holy Port'. Zarco's ship, however, beached somewhere near the present site of Vila Baleira, between two rivers which still run to its sandy shore.

One of these small rivers reaches the sea running through the edge of this tiny town. Its cobbled streets centre on the plaza where the island's first church, with pointed clock and bell-tower, dominates the triangular 'square'. This church, Nossa Senhora da Piedade, was built in the late fifteenth century and is one of the island's oldest buildings. The historic church stands in front of the island's most famous house, the island home of Christopher Columbus.

When the newly-discovered islands of Madeira were divided between governors, a Bartholomeu Perestrello was given command of Porto Santo in 1420. Entrusted to develop the island, he instigated the construction of the church and established the first settlement near to where Zarco had landed. Of interest to historians and art-lovers, a seventeenth-century painting of Mary Magdelene at Christ's feet forms the centre-piece in Porto Santo's ancient church.

Visiting Funchal, on Madeira, on a trading mission, the celebrated navigator, Christopher Columbus, sailed across to Porto Santo, met its elderly governor and, more importantly, fell in love with his daughter, Isabel Moniz. Married in the island's new church, the couple stayed on Porto Santo for some weeks before honeymooning in Funchal. The little red-tiled cottage where Columbus and Isabel stayed during 1479 is located in Rua Cristovão Colombo, named after the explorer. Rua Colombo No. 12 is now a museum to the island's famous 'son'. On the corner of the street near to Columbus's cottage is an ancient jailhouse and, across the square, is the town's public drinking fountain, widely known for the mineral content of its stream-fresh water.

A promenade runs along the beach-head and a jetty services local fishing boats and ferries from Funchal. Most of Porto Santo's little streets are named after famous personalities and its two discoverers. Just behind the esplanade, Avenida Dr Manuel Pestana Junior, there is a Tourist Information Office. A number of attractive old houses, draped in colourful oleander or bougainvillea, the two-storey Town Hall with its grandiose frontage, the Chapels of Grace, the Holy Spirit and St Peter, are the sum historic interests in Porto Santo.

For the young and active visitors, there are two discotheques in the town. The main restaurant is the Baiana and, next door, there is a cinema on Rua Dr Nuno S. Teixeira. The two main hotels are Porto Santo and Praia Dourada and the town has three pensions, Palmeiras, the Central and the Zarco. Taxis can be hired in Porto Santo as can bicycles and even donkeys, but there is no car hire on the island. Buses run a regular service to the airport and Camacha. Other routes across the island are intermittent. Three travel agencies, Blandy, Abratour and Star all have offices near the town centre.

ELSEWHERE ON THE ISLAND

COAST EXCURSION

As transport on the island consists of hiking, bicycling, donkey, taxi, or the erratic bus service, time should be allowed to enjoy the two main island tours. Some visitors may also want to include a boat trip or fishing excursion offered from the island's main jetty at Porto Santo.

Travelling out of Porto Santo (Vila Baleira) there are several opportunities for a day's excursion but most visitors come for the glorious beach. Taking the beachfront road, Avenida Henrique Vieira de Castro, south-west out of town, a little stream is crossed before skirting the Lombas lookout on the right of the road. From this low hill there is a good view back across the town and west to the airport.

Campo de Cima
The village of Pedras Pretas is passed, or one could take refreshment at the Gazela Restaurant at nearby Campo de Cima. Look for the ancient and picturesque windmill on the nearby hill.

Campo de Baixo
A little further on, at Campo de Baixo, see the little drinking fountain, typical of several on the island. The tiny Chapel of Espirito Santé can be seen just to the right of the road. Accommodation is also available at the pension on the beautiful, clean beach. Look for the Chapel of St Peter up in the ravine to the west of the coastal road. In order to see the best part of the long beach and end up with a midday meal one should keep on along the shoreline road, past another small pension at Cabeco do Ponta.

Cabeco do Ponta
The Mariazinha restaurant and bar here at Ponta serve excellent fresh seafood.

Ponta da Calheta
Around a vast, sandy beach the road leads to Ponta da Calheta, famed for its black volcanic basalt rocks, its reef-strewn channel separating the main island from Baixo Islet, and its seafood restaurant, the Estrela da Calheta (The Star of Calheta). Try also the Toca do Pescador restaurant. This beach is one of the most popular and built-up on the island. Just a short hike away from the beach is a great lookout point with views of the rocky, indented coastline and the ocean. This part of the coastline is celebrated as being one of the best fishing grounds on the island. Just behind the rocky shore is another of the island's several fountains. There are some pleasant walks around the southern point of Porto Santo and a few hilly tracks have been established. Note the attempts to terrace parts of hillsides in order to make the

Terraced hillsides

most of the sparse rainfall – when it does come. Drought has been a particular problem on the island over the past few years. Between Ponta da Calheta and the centrally-located airport there is little else of interest apart from the arid, desert landscape and the ever-present summit of the Pico de Ana Ferreira, at 980 ft. (295 m.) the highest of the three rugged peaks in this part of the island.

NORTHERN TOUR

Back in the main town another tour which makes a day's outing is the northern circuit. Taking the riverside, **Rua Brigadeiro Couceiro** route, a continuation of Columbus Street, out of Porto Santo, the road passes the airport terminal on the left, crossing numerous gullies on the way to Camacha.

Castle Mountain – Pico do Castelo
To the right of the road is the Pico do Castelo (Castle Mountain) 1,443 ft. (437 m.), has a lookout point on the left of the road, from which, on good days, Madeira island is visible to the south. This wood-covered mountain was once the retreat of islanders escaping bands of marauding pirates in earlier centuries. Several rusted cannon and rocks strewn

on the table-topped, volcanic cone are all the evidence left of the ancient fortress of more violent days. It is easier to reach Pico do Castelo by taking the Rua Schiapa de Azevedo road out of Porto Santo, or forking off onto the conifer-lined route from the airport road at Dragoal. For refreshment there is the Estufas restaurant at Dragoal.

Camacha
In Camacha itself, there are two good restaurants, the Torres and the Estrella do Norte. From here there are several opportunities for the explorer. To the east the Pico do Facho (Beacon Mountain) at 1,676 ft. (511 m.), domi-nates the landscape and is the island's highest peak. During buccaneering days the islanders of Porto Santo used to warn the Madeirans of approaching raiders by lighting a great beacon on the summit of Pico do Facho.

Porto das Eiras
A short trip to the north of Camacha the road leads over ravines to the rugged coast at a bay known as Porto das Eiras.

Fountain in the Sands – Fonte da Areia
Heading due west from Camacha another road leads to the famous Fonte da Areia, (the Fountain in the Sands). Here the weird cliffs have been eroded to reveal a strange variety of coloured strata, deep caves and precipices. The waterfall here is popular with the local people who collect water from the stream and wash clothes in the deep pool.

Serra de Dentro
Continuing on the north ring road a fascinating tour through hills, patchwork fields, wooded outcrops and deep riverbeds takes the visitor around the lower slopes of the conical Pico do Facho and the Pico da Cabrita (Goat Mountain) at 1,640 ft. (500 m.) to the little village of Serra de Dentro. The two high mountains to the left are Pico das Urzes and Pico Branco.

Serra de Fora
From here the road continues to the village of Serra de Fora and here there is a welcome restaurant and bar, the Teodorico. One of the island's highest mountains, Pico do Concelmo is on the left. After Serra de Fora look out for the

Rocha de Nossa Senhora (the Rock of Our Lady) to the right, after the turning on the left to the fishing port of Porto dos Frades. Also to the right of the road is the little Capela, or Chapel, da Gracia. Right on the easternmost point of the island, opposite Cima Islet, are the twin mountains of Pico dos Macaricos, 970 ft. (285 m.) and Pico de Baito, 660 ft. (206 m.).

Portela

A short drive from Porto Santo, to the east, along Estrada de Serra Fora, around the pretty Valé do Touro, Portela is one of the island's easiest-reached attractions. If the north circular route has been taken, then Portela is the last stop-over beauty spot on the day's outing. This location is both a lookout, from which one can see the great arc of beach running down to Ponta de Calheta in the far south, and a fine beach. There is one of the island's only working windmills on the hillside at Portela and, down on the coast, is the little village of Penedo.

Porto de Abrigo

If one continues along the beach from Penedo, east, away from Porto Santo, one will come to Porto de Abrigo, an important fishing harbour in the shadow of Pico do Macarico. It is sometimes possible to take fishing trips or boat excursions from Porto de Abrigo.

GAZETTEER

The following describes more than one hundred of the towns, villages, hamlets, estates, sights and sites, of the Madeiran archipelago. A brief description is given of each.

AEROPORTOS There are two airports in Madeira. The main one is Santa Catarina Airport, built in 1964 and located on the south-east of the main island, between Machico and Santa Cruz. Porto Santo also has an airport situated in the centre of the island and built in 1960 as a reserve NATO airfield. TAP Air Portugal serves both airports on scheduled flights and there are many charter lines which fly to Madeira.

ÁGUA DE PENA This is the name given to a modern holiday village located in the east of Madeira near Santa Catarina airport.

ÁGUAS MANUS The 'Water of the Mansion', a crossing of the Levada do Pico in spectacular wooded landscape overlooking a deep valley, at the eastern end of the long mountain ridge which traverses Madeira.

ARCO DE SÃO JORGE This village suffered a landslide in 1689 and, although the houses were shifted, all of them remarkably remained intact. Set on a point almost midway along Madeira's north coastline, this

little village is surrounded by viewpoints from which the stunning cliff-lined coast can be viewed like the Ponta de São Jorge.

ASSOMADA Located near the coastal road as it skirts the Cabo Garajau, this is a small hamlet.

BABOSAS A little hamlet just to the east of Monte. Note the tiny white chapel set into the wooded hillside, with its twin belfries.

BAIA DE ZARCO Recently named for the benefit of tourists, this bay encompasses a stretch of coastline which curves around the south-east corner of Madeira, in the lee of the Peninsula de São Lourenço. Named after the discoverer who first landed here, the bay is centred on Machico.

BALCOES This is a lookout near Ribeiro Frio in the Metade Valley located in the centre of the island north of Funchal.

BICA DA CANA The 'Spout of the Cane Sugar', betrays in its name the fame the island's 'white gold' production had in past centuries. This high, wooded region on the Levada de Serra probably got its name from the sugar trade which was so prevalent on Madeira. This area lies in the middle of the western sector of the island, to the east of the Pául de Serra plateau.

BOA MORTE A wooded region on the Levada do Norte, just to the north-east of Ribeira Brava near the south coast of Madeira.

BOA NOVA Just to the north west of Funchal, on the Camancha road, this is the site of a modern church which incorporates the ruins of a seventeenth-century convent.

BOAVENTURA A little town of about 3,000 people, this settlement is set centrally on the island's north coast and specialises in producing willow wands for Madeira's famous wicker-work. Terraces cover the rounded slopes of this region which is perched high above the sea.

BOCA DE ENCUMEADA This well-known beauty spot is located in the centre of the island between Ribiera Brava and São Vicente, about 3,300 feet (1000 m.) up in the central massif.

CABO GARAJUA One of the southernmost points on Madeira, in the eastern part of the island around the coast from Funchal, also known as Ponta da Garajua. The statue of Christ here is a smaller version of that in Rio de Janeiro.

CABO GIRÃO This almost vertical cliff, plunges down 1,933 feet (589 m.) to the sea, and pocket-handkerchief plots of green cultivation cling to its reddish flank, carved out by the remarkable tenacity of Madeiran

farmers. A lookout point has been fenced in for visitors to enjoy the sheer majesty of the world's second highest sea cliff.

CALHETA This port on the south-west coast is reached by a steep road down from the main coastal route and has a population of about 4,000. Agriculture here concentrates mainly on bananas and wine production. The village church was rebuilt in 1639 and has a carved wooden ceiling. Treasures in the church include an ebony and silver tabernacle donated by King Manuel I. Another church, the Nossa Senhora de Loreto, lies a short walk from this busy little fishing village.

CAMANCHA A small town on the road running from Funchal to Porto da Cruz with a population of about 7,000, this centrally-located settlement is famous for its wickerwork. Several wickerwork factories in the town can be visited to watch the willow osiers being steamed and woven into a variety of utensils and decorative objects. Visitors are often entertained by local folk dances here.

CÂMARA DE LOBOS The Câmara, or Gorge, was named after the 'sea wolves' or seals which frequented this spot on the south coast of Madeira. Some stories suggest it was the proliferation of 'wolf-fish' or sea perch which Zarco found in the waters off this coast which gave this pretty village its name. The full name, Câmara de Lobos, means the 'Gorge of the Wolves'. Favourite with painters, notably Sir Winston Churchill when he visited Madeira in 1950, this picturesque little fishing port sports whitewashed houses and bright red roofs, doll-like against the great cliffs which shelter its little harbour. On the seafront is a tiny white chapel, built in the late fifteenth century and reconstructed in 1723. The village has a population of around 1,500 and is famous for the embroidery school established in the village.

CAMPANÁRIO This little village west of the Câmara de Lobos, along the coast road and by the Levada do Norte, has an interesting seventeenth-century parish church.

CANHAS Pretty little village on the south-west coast road between Ponta do Sol and Calheta. Fourteen statues on the roadside represent the Stations of the Cross.

CANIÇAL Located on the narrow promontory of Madeira which points out to the east, this south-facing port was a thriving whaling station and still produces cetacea oil. There is a small beach, Prainha, below the village and, above the stream, is the Nossa Senhora da Piedade, Our Lady of Piety, hermitage.

CANIÇO Built on the Rio Caniço, inland from the cliffs of the south-east coast, this town of about 8,000 inhabitants has an interesting sixteenth-century chapel, the Madre de Dues 'Mother of the Twins' – possibly connected with the first two children born on Madeira, the twins Adam and Eva. There is also an eighteenth-century parish church here.

CHÃO DOS LOUROS 'Ground of the Laurels'. Located in the centre of the island to the south of Rosario, this is no more than a tiny agricultural hamlet.

CHOUPANA Tiny settlement to the east of Monte just above the capital, Funchal.

CRISTA DE GALO 'Cock's Comb' hamlet, named after the striking mountain pinnacle which resembles a crest, just west of the Pousada at Vinhaticos, central Madeira.

CURRAL DAS FREIRAS Literally the 'Hideaway of the Nuns', this remote and secluded spot, in the crater of an extinct volcano, was chosen as a refuge by the nuns of the Convento de Santa Clara, Funchal's fifteenth-century convent. In 1566, when French pirates razed the coastal settlements, the nuns were alerted and fled to this almost inaccessible flat crater surrounded by its high mountainous walls. Today the small village on the site is one of the most isolated anywhere and some residents have not even ventured beyond their protective, rocky crater. A levada runs from this village to the outskirts of Funchal and the walk along its banks provides an insight into the nature of the Madeiran countryside.

CURRAL DOS ROMEIROS The 'Pilgrims Hideout' and an historical location where devout monks hid away from the ravages of pirates and buccaneers during the periods of pillage from the fifteenth to the seventeenth century. Not far north of Funchal, in

Curral das Freias – the 'Hideaway of the Nuns'

the lower slopes of the mountains.

EIRA DO SERRADO The terrace of Serrado is a path from where there are breathtaking views of the extinct volcano crater and its tiny village of Curral das Freiras. The panoramic pathway skirts the peak of Pico do Serrado.

ENCUMEANDA The abbreviated version of Boca da Encumeada.

ESTREITO DA CALHETA Down in the south-west corner of the island, this spot is famous for its sixteenth-century chapel, the Capela dos Resi Magos – the Chapel of the Three Kings with its fine ceiling, triptych and decorated woodwork.

ESTREITO DE CÂMARA DE LOBOS The 'Narrows of the Gorge of Wolves' is a small village of some 1,200 inhabitants widely known for the fine quality of its wine. The little church here has a remarkably ornate interior compared to its blank, whitewashed outside walls. Note the cradle vault and baroque-style chandeliers.

FAIAL Sometimes known as São Roque do Faial, this little town of less than 1,000 people overlooks the rocky north east coast and is set on a wide, flat plain between two valleys and overshadowed by the Penha d'Águia, Eagle Rock mountain. A large white church, with tall, tiered and pointed belfry stands out on the hillside against the backdrop of vineyards, sugar cane, willow groves and cattle sheds.

FAJÃ DA OVELHA Literally, the 'Sheep Pasture', situated on the south-west coastal road, this tiny village is set in woodland and overshadowed by a mountainous wall of rock.

FONTE DA AREIA Famous sight on the island of Porto Santo, on the north-west coast, known as the 'Fountain of the Sands'.

FONTE DO BISPO The 'Bishop's Fountain', located at the height of the ridge in the western part of the island, a spectacular lookout and picnic area.

FUNCHAL The capital city and port of the entire Madeiran archipelago with a population of almost 50,000 and situated on a horseshoe bay in the south of Madeira island. Many famous sites and historic buildings.

GARAJAU Short for the Cabo, or the Ponta da Garajau, a headland in the south of Madeira.

GINJAS Agricultural hamlet in the north-central part of Madeira north of Rosário. Note the acres of terraced fields dotted with tiny thatched huts.

ILHAS DESERTAS Three uninhabited, desert islands: Deserta Grande, Ilhéu de Bugio, 'Monkey Isle', and Ilhéu Chao, the 'Soily Island'. All three lie in a group about 11 miles (17 kms.) to the south-west of Madeira.

ILHAS SELVAGENS Five small islets make up this desert island group known as the 'Wild Isles' lying about 170 miles (280 kms.) due south of Madeira.

ILHÉU DE BAIXO One of the larger of Porto Santo's satellite islands, located off Ponta da Calheta in the south.

ILHÉU DO GUINCHO 'Isle of the Animal's Shriek' – a curious name for this tiny islet off the north of the peninsula of Ponta da São Lourenço, in the far east of the island of Madeira.

ILHÉU DA RIBEIRA DA JANELA Spectacular basalt stack set in the sea off the town of Ribeira da Janela on the north-west tip of Madeira, outstanding from its two accompanying

Faial village in the north of Madeira

stacks in that it is pierced with a 'janelo', or window.

JARDIM DE SERRA A famous beauty spot located up in the mountains inland from the south coast road.

JARDIM DO MAR A beauty spot on the south coast near the town of Calheta.

JOÃO FRINO Tiny agricultural hamlet on the Levada da Serra in the eastern part of Madeira.

LAMACEIROS Tiny agricultural region in the central part of eastern Madeira.

*LEVADAS Levadas is the local name for the canals, waterways and channels which bring precious water down from the mountain heights, slowly dispensing it on all levels, to the terraces, or poios, before entering the stream and river networks. They date back some 250 or more years and were mostly constructed by slave labour. Almost 620 miles (1,000 kms.) of irrigation channels criss-cross the landscape of Madeira and most have footpaths which give the visitor access to the interior of the island. Famous levadas include those of TORNOS, FURADO, CURRAL and SERRA, near to Funchal; the levadas of CALHETA, VINTE E CINCO FONTES, RABAÇAL, NORTES and SERRA, in the west; and the levadas of MACHICO-CANIÇAL and TORNOS in the east.

LOMBADA DA PONTA DO SOL Famous for its church,

the Capela do Santo Espirito, or Holy Spirit, this chapel was founded by João Esmeraldo, the friend that Christopher Columbus stayed with on Madeira. Although it was established in the late fifteenth century, this chapel was rebuilt 300 years later in 1720. A house in the village bears Esmeraldo's coat of arms.

LORETO A small church stands here overlooking the south coast and there are a number of interesting, red-tiled and gaily-painted buildings lining the narrow streets. Visit the local agricultural produce market.

MACHICO Madeira's second most important town with a population of nearly 12,000. This fine port was said to be named after the Englishman Robert Machim who, legend has it, was shipwrecked here in 1344. Together with his lover, Machim was buried under a cedar tree and the explorer Zarco is said to have found the grave. The new governor of this part of the island, Zarco's co-discoverer, Tristão Vas Teixeira, then built a chapel, the Chapel of Miracles, over the site in 1420. The church which now stands on the spot was reconstructed in the nineteenth century after floods destroyed the original in 1803. A statue of Teixeira stands outside the clock-towered church. A cedar-wood cross displayed in the chapel was said to have been found floating at sea by a Robert Page in 1829 and he claimed that it was the original erected over Machim's grave almost 500 years earlier – hence the 'miracle'. The doorway to the side of the chapel

Machico

was presented by King Manuel I. The Capela de São Roque, another church built in the late fifteenth century by Teixeira, has a fine ceiling, interesting religious paintings and *azuljeo* tiling; note the statue of the Virgin over the High Altar which was donated by King Manuel I. The bay on which the town is built is overlooked by a triangular fortress dating from 1706.

MAGDALENA DO MAR On the south coast, in the western half of the island, this is a belvedere overlooking a small beach far below the lookout terrace. There are a few pretty little houses tucked into the hillside here.

MARMELEIROS Located up in the hills north of Funchal, this is a well-known lookout, or terrace balcony with spectacular views of the capital.

MATUR Another name for the tourist complex of Ponta da Queimada.

MIRADOURO DO JUNCAL Surrounding the imposing peak of Juncal, a pathway affords fantastic views to the north and east coasts.

MIRADOURO DO PICO ARIEIRO On the summit of Pico Arieiro, at almost 6,000 feet (1,820 m.), a lookout has been built, giving a rewarding panorama to those climbing the centrally-located peak.

MIRADOURO DO PINÁCULO Just a short walk from

Funchal, this high point is a particularly spectacular lookout spot. A pergola covers the lookout point.

MIRADOURO FRANCISCO ÁLVARES NOBREGA A famous beauty spot from where panoramic views over Zarco Bay and the peninsula of Ponta São Lourenço attract visitors to this specially-designed belvedere named after a late eighteenth-century Portuguese poet.

MONTE With the short, and to the point name of 'Mountain' this town of about 8,000 population is famed for its church, the Nossa Sẽnhora do Monte, founded in 1470 but rebuilt at the end of the eighteenth century. The first two children to be born on Madeira, Adam Gonçalves Ferreira and his twin sister, Eva, are said to have erected the first chapel on this site. A jewelled statue of Madeira's patron saint, Our Lady of the mountain, displayed in the church, was found during the fifteenth century at Terreiro da Luta, the site of a miraculous appearance of the Virgin. Emperor Karl I of Austria, whose tomb lies in the church, lived in the Quinta do Monte during his exile from 1921 until his death the following year. Some treasures donated by his Empress, Zita, are displayed in the sacristy. This church is the centre of an annual pilgrimage. The great stairway outside the handsome church, 68 steps, is the departure point for traditional toboggan runs down into the capital of Funchal. In the town square is the 1906 Chapel of Nossa Sẽnhora da Conceicao. Set in plane tree groves this mountain location was once a popular health spa. The views from Monte, across Funchal are spectacular.

PARQUE DAS QUEIMADAS Just outside the town of Santana, at the foot of the Ruivo mountains this botanical park makes an attractive detour from the north coast road. Visit the Junta Geral shelter here.

PAÚL DA SERRA This great plateau is one of the major geological features of Madeira and lies around 4,655 feet (1,420 m.) up in the centre of the western half of the island. This land, often marshy, is now being developed as pasture.

PAÚL DO MAR This little fishing village lies on the southwestern coast of Madeira and supports a fish canning factory. A zig-zag pathway leads from the beachside village up to the coastal road.

PENHA DE ÁGUIA 'Eagle Rock' is a vast massif, a towering crag which dominates the surrounding countryside near Faial, on the north-east facing coast. This is one of Madeira's best-known beauty spots and photographic subjects.

PICO DAS PEDRAS 'Rocky Mountain' is a popular picnic spot up in the mountains inland from the town of Santana.

PICO DO ARIEIRO At 5,940 feet (1,810 m.), this is Madeira's third highest peak. A road runs to the summit and

Penha D'Águia – 'Eagle Rock'

there is a pathway which links this mountain with Pico Ruivo. It is a good five-hour walk there and back.

PICO DO CASTELO One of the island of Porto Santo's best known peaks where islanders once sought refuge from pirates. Literally 'Castle Peak', note the ruins of an ancient fortress.

PICO DO FACHO Located in the centre of the north-eastern part of the island of Porto Santo, this is its highest peak, Pico do Facho (Beacon Peak) at 1,696 ft. (517 m.).

PICO DO JORGE One of Madeira's highest mountains, this peak rises to around 5,515 feet (1,692 m.).

PICO DAS TORRES The jagged 'Peak of Towers' is Madeira's second highest mountain at 6,075 feet (1,851 m.), and is located in the group of high peaks in the centre of the island north of Funchal.

PICO CIDRAO Another magnificent mountain in the group which includes Madeira's highest peaks, this outcrop overlooks the Curral das Freiras and is 5,912 feet (1,802 m.) high.

PICO DOS BARCELOS At nearly 1,200 feet (364 m.) high, this peak affords fantastic views from its lookout point, surrounded by tropical flowers, over the south coast and surrounding countryside.

PICO GRANDE One of Madeira's more spectacular peaks at 5,275 feet (1,608 m.).

PICO RUIVO For the energetic who wish to climb the island's highest point, the 'Red Peak', at 6,106 feet (1,861 m.), the rewards are panoramic views across the surrounding mountains and gorges of this centrally-located volcanic pinnacle.

PICO SERRATO 'Sawtooth' mountain is situated north-west of Funchal, up in the mountains. This peak sits in the centre of a beauty spot. For magnificent views across the central 'backbone' range of mountains running across the island from west to east, this must be the best. At 3,318 feet (1,060 m.), this peak forms the tip of the famous lookout point of the Eira do Serrado, the Terrace of Serrado.

POISO PASS Wild moorland and 4,633 feet (1,412 m.) up, this pass makes a favourite walk in the centre of the mountains north of Funchal. There is a restaurant here, a few scattered houses and some excellent picnic spots.

PONTA DA CALHETA This is one of the island of Porto Santo's famous landmarks and is located on the southern tip of the island. There is an interesting seventeenth-century chapel here.

PONTA DA QUIEMADA Also known as Matur, this is Madeira's largest tourist complex situated near the airport and Machico on the south-east coast.

PONTA DA OLIVEIRA A forty-minute bus ride east of Funchal, this point lies on Madeira's south-eastern coast and there is a good hotel and restaurant here.

PONTA DE GARAJAU Also known as Cabo Garajau, this south-facing headland is famed for its miniature of Rio de Janeiro's 'Christ of the Rock', erected by villagers in 1927.

PONTA DELGADA The 'Narrow Point' is located in the centre of Madeira's rocky north coast. This village of around 2,000 inhabitants is set high up

over the sea crashing on rocks far below and has a seawater swimming pool. Its little church, colonial houses and narrow streets make the village setting quite photogenic.

PONTA DAS GAVIOTAS In English this name means 'Gull Point', a well-deserved tag for the hundreds of seabirds which swoop around this south-facing cliffs. The ancient fossil beds here are an attraction for fossil hunters and for scientists the world over and provide an intimate knowledge of the island of Madeira in ancient times from the thousands of prehistoric remnants of early plant and animal life which have been discovered in the rocks on this point. This is a popular stop-over for walkers on the peninsula of Ponta de São Lourenço.

PONTA DA SÃO JORGE A lookout near São Jorge on the north coast.

PONTA DE SÃO LOURENÇO The easternmost tip of the island of Madeira, which forms a long peninsula. There is a lighthouse on this point and fossil-hunters are attracted to the extensive prehistoric deposits in the reddish soil which is found on the peninsula. Beauty spots here include Prainha Beach, Ponta das Gaviotas, Abra Bay and Ponta do Buraco.

PONTA DO BURACO 'Hole Point' is an important lookout on the south side of the Ponta de São Lourenço, the eastern peninsula of Madeira. This is a famous lookout, with views to the east over the extreme end of the island, south towards the Ilhas Desertas and east over the fossil cliffs of Ponta das Gaviotas.

PONTA DO PARGO
'Dolphin Point', allegedly named after a giant dolphin which Zarco's sailors netted in one of their exploratory voyages. Built just inland from the westernmost tip of Madeira where the important lighthouse is located, this little village supports a fishing community.

PONTA DO SOL
A tiny village set among the south coast cliffs on the river of the same name. 'Sunny Point' has a fifteenth-century church, the Nossa Sênhora da Luz 'Our Lady of Light' – fittingly! The finely-decorated ceiling in the parish church and the religious regalia on display is worth viewing. Even more historic is the nearby Capela do Santo Espirito, at Lombada da Ponta do Sol, a chapel founded by João Esmeraldo, the friend that Christopher Columbus stayed with on Madeira. Although it was established in the late fifteenth century, this chapel was rebuilt 300 years later. The ruins near here are those of the home of Flemish sugar baron, Jean d'Esmenaut, who founded the village in the fifteenth century. The local church of São João is of architectural and historic interest.

PORTELA
On Porto Santo, on the southern bay, this coastal viewpoint is a famous tourist attraction overlooking a spectacular arc of sandy beach.

PORTELA PASS
In the eastern sector of the island this spectacular viewpoint is situated inland from the north coast and provides fine vistas of both the north and south coasts.

PORTO DA CRUZ
On the north-east coast, this little port has a small, dark, volcanic beach and is surrounded by craggy cliffs. The population is around 4,000. The church here is one of the few modern churches on the island.

PORTO MONIZ
Another tiny fishing village of around 300 people situated on the north-westernmost tip of the island on the main coast road. The little islet, with its few fishermen's cottages, a short distance offshore is called the Ilhéu Mole. The harbour here is one of the best on the rocky north coast and it is possible to bathe in the sea-washed rock pools. The narrow, cobbled streets and quaint old houses are a picture not to be missed.

PORTO SANTO (ILHA DO)
The second largest island in the Madeiran archipelago. A total of 3,200 people live on this $7\frac{1}{2}$ mile (12 km.) long and 4 mile (6 km.) wide island lying about 27 miles (40 kms.) north-east of Madeira. The island has a port and an airport.

PORTO SANTO
This is the largest town on the island of Porto Santo, population around 2,000, and is also known as Vila Baleira. Its famous sites are the church, Nossa Sênhora da Piedade, which was built in the late fifteenth century and is one of the

island's oldest buildings. This historic church stands in front of the island's most famous house, the island home of Christopher Columbus.

POUSADAS Portuguese government-run hotels situated in beauty spots or locations of historic interest are known as Pousadas. There are only two Pousadas on Madeira, situated in the centre of the island and these are the Pousada do Arierio which is located high up in the Pico do Arieiro mountains north of Funchal, and the Pousada dos Vinháticos, situated north-west of Funchal on the route to Encumeada.

PRAINHA The last hamlet on the Ponta de São Lourenço and Madeira's easternmost settlement. The church here is the Nossa Sēnhora da Piedade, Our Lady of Piety, and the black sandy beach here is the only real

A local villager

beach on Madeira's main island.

PRAZERES A small village overlooking the Levada Caleta-Ponta do Pargo on the south-west corner of Madeira. The flat agricultural part of this area, with its white-painted houses dotted among the crops, contrasts sharply with the nearby jagged crags, themselves etched with terraces. Prazeres, aptly, means 'The Pleasures'.

QUINTA BOM SUCESSO The 'Good Times Mansion': in its grounds the Madeiran authorities have laid out the island's celebrated Jardim Botanico, or Botanical Gardens, designed on spectacular terraces overlooking Funchal.

QUINTA DA JUNTA Old country house in Santo Antonio da Serra, once owned by the Blandy family.

QUINTA DA PALMIERA The 'Palm Tree Mansion' is located to the north of Funchal. Set on a steep escarpment at the end of a short path, this private residence is built on a terrace overlooking the capital. A Gothic-style window forms a gazebo on the lawns and is said to date from the late fifteenth century, some say it came from the house in which Christopher Columbus stayed.

QUINTA DA POMAR The 'Mansion of the Orchard' is located to the east of Monte, just north of Funchal. One of the many great country houses, this Quinta has a magnificent view-point across the valley of the João Gomez river which runs down to

the capital of Madeira.

QUINTA DO PALHEIRA FERREIRO Often called the Palheiro Ferriero, or 'Haystack Mansion of the Blacksmith', this is a private park just outside Funchal, open to public viewing. The floral gardens here are magnificently laid out in formal designs with topiaried trees contrasting with ancient dragon trees, wild palms and great tree ferns.

QUINTA DO TIL Just north of Funchal, this is a private Quinta but has an interesting gateway.

QUINTA GRANDE A typical country mansion and estate located on the south coast road just to the west of Câmara de Lobos and on the road which runs north of the great cliff of Cabo Girão.

RABAÇAL Located in the centre of the western part of the island, this small village is famous for its 250-year-old levada which leads to the *Vinte e Cinco Fontes* – the Twenty-five Fountains.

RAPOSEIRA Situated on the Levada Calheta-Ponta do Pargo, in the south-west of the island. A small agricultural village not far from the coastal road. Cereals are grown on the rolling slopes in this area.

RIBEIRA BRAVA This small village is named after the River Ribeira Brava, or 'Wild River'. Located at the mouth of the Brava on the south coast, this port has a seventeenth-century

Sea sports

fortress, a sixteenth-century parish church with an *azueljos*-tiled belfry roof and a picturesque village square. There is also a small beach here. This is the site for the St Peter Festival which takes place in June.

RIBEIRA DA JANELA The Janela river, in the north-west corner of Madeira, runs through the outskirts of this village which gets its name from the natural 'window' in the basalt stack known as the Ilhéu da Ribiera da Janela. Janela is Portuguese for 'window'. Two other massive volcanic rocks on one side of the river's mouth give the spot a surrealistic atmosphere.

RIBEIRA DO INFERNO Spectacular scenery sets off the course of this 'River of Hell' which, in the rains, thunders through its narrow gorge to the sea below.

RIBEIRA DOS SOCORRI- DOS Located inland, and north of the Câmara de Lobos the 'River of the Survivors' was

named after those few early fifteenth-century settlers who, trapped when the island was set on fire, took refuge in this river until they were rescued.

RIBEIRO FRIO The government have established a trout hatchery in the waters of the 'Cold River', there is a special botanical garden here and a small hotel. The levada walk is one of the most popular on the island.

RISCO FALLS A famous beauty spot near the *Vinte e Cinco Fontes* high in the east part of Madeira. A levada is named after both of these sights.

ROSÁRIO One of the island's many pretty villages located in the valley of the São Vicente river north of the 'saddle' in Madeira's mountain range. It has a lovely stream running by and a little church.

SALGADOS An estate inland near Camacha, known for its willow production.

SANTA Short for Santa

Maria Madalena. Also a pension in the extreme north-eastern end of the island of Madeira. This small hotel is located near the town of Porto Moniz.

SANTA CRUZ This small village set on an attractive bay on the south-east side of the island has a sixteenth-century church built in 1533, São Salvador, the island's oldest original church. It also has an early sixteenth-century Câmara Municipal, or Town Hall. The church contains several interesting tombs and typical *azulejos* tile work which came originally from the nearby monastery.

SANTA MARIA MADAL-ENA Site of a chapel with a curious spire.

SANTANA Instantly recognisable from pictures of its curious, thatched and gaily-painted houses, this town of 5,000 people is a regional capital and situated inland from the rugged north coast cliffs. Fertile and productive, the land in this part of Madeira is considered the best for horticulturalists.

SANTO ANTONIO DA SERRA 'Saint Anthony of the Mountain' is often abbreviated to Santo da Serra. The pretty eighteenth-century church in typically baroque style is the main attraction of this town of some 2,000 people. The other, modern attraction is the island's only golf course of 9 holes (2,622 yds.) which looks out over the north-east coastline. The Quinta da Junta Park was once owned by the well-known Blandy family. Eucalyptus and mimosa copses

extent from thick forested regions surrounding the town, and the comparatively flat landscape of this valley is dotted with areas of pasture.

SANTO DA SERRA The shortened version of Santo Antonio da Serra.

SÃO ANTONIO Short for Santo Antonio da Serra.

SÃO JORGE With a population of almost 3,000, this small town has an interesting and elaborately decorated church, São Jorge, built in the seventeenth century. The town's location, on the high cliffs in a central position on the north coast, overlooks a lighthouse.

SÃO MARTINHO This village of around 170 people, located in the south of the eastern sector of Madeira, just west of Funchal, is remembered for its tiny chapel situated on a little mount. Tiny it may seem from the outside, but the church's interior is extraordinarily large.

SÃO ROQUE DO FAIAL The lengthy version of Faial, literally the 'Safe Castle of Faial' although no castle now stands here.

SÃO VICENTE St Vincent is located on the north coast and has a population of 5,500. This pretty little village was overrun by a landslide in 1928 and today it serves as a base for mountaineers taking on the surrounding peaks. Note the painting on the roof of the parish chuch – São Vicente. The chapel on a hillock is to Our Lady of Fâtima, built in

1952. Just outside the village is a strange chapel hollowed out of a rock overlooking the sea.

SEIXAL   Really no more than a hamlet, this tiny settlement is devoted to wine production. Spectacular waterfalls add to the stunning scenery in this north-west coastal village.

SERRA DE AGUA   North of Ribeira Brava, on the River Brava, this little village has a population of about 1,500.

TÁBUA   Small estate inland from the south coast on the Ribeira Brava just north of the coastal village.

TERREIRO   DA   LUTA From this high location the views across Monte to Funchal and the wide sweep of its bay are stupendous. This is where the statue of Our Lady of the Mountain, now in Monte's church, was found in the fifteenth century, and where a shepherdess is said to have had a miraculous vision. In 1927, after suffering continued bombardment from German submarines during the 1914–18 World War, the Bishop had a monument erected to Our Lady of Peace. The tiny population manually hauled the chains now decorating the statue, all the way up from Funchal harbour where they had been retrieved

from ships sunk during the siege. This is Madeira's largest monument. There is a tiny chapel in this little village which is set in peaceful woodland. From here, visitors can take a toboggan run down the steep road into Monte.

VALÉ   DO   PARAISO 'Paradise Valley' to the east of Funchal and a favourite beauty and picnic spot.

VILA BALEIRA   Alternative name for the main town on the island of Porto Santo, Porto Santo itself.

VINHÁTICOS   Agricultural estate and location of the government Pousada, or country hotel.

VINTE E CINCO FONTES Twenty-five Springs is a famous beauty spot and is located in the centre of the western half of Madeira. This picturesque valley is more of a deep gorge, carpeted in   vegetation.   Half-moon shaped, the gorge into which the springs cascade is lined with ferns but, of the original 25 falls, a number have been channelled into the nearby levada.

VITÓRIA   Located above the Ribeira dos Socorridos, it is a short walk from this tiny village overlooking the south coast to the famous Câmara de Lobos.

The symbol used throughout this book is based on one of Madeira's most popular flowers. The 'Bird of Paradise Flower' – Ave do Paraiso (*Strelitzia reginae*) grows throughout the year on the island and has become synonymous with the abundant flora on this 'Floating Garden of the Ocean'.

INDEX

Other Windrush Island Guides

MENORCA   John and Margaret Goulding

Menorca, most northerly of the Balearic Islands and the least dedicated to tourism, has long been a favourite destination for the discriminating holidaymaker. Its pleasant climate, pastoral countryside, gracious cities and superb beaches (many of them remote and little visited) make it ideal for a relaxing yet interesting holiday. Additional attractions are the island's fascinatingly varied history and its uniquely spectacular megalithic monuments.

But Menorca also offers lively modern resorts with a high standard of holiday accommodation. In this, the fullest guide to the island yet published, over seventy beaches are described in detail. In addition to chapters on history, flora and fauna, sports and eating out, it provides a wealth of practical advice to enable the visitor to enjoy the charm and variety of Menorca to the full.

£6.95   ISBN 0 900075 46 5   *Fully Illustrated*

LANZAROTE   John and Margaret Goulding

Lanzarote is the closest of the Canary Islands to Africa. Consequently, thousands of visitors are attracted to its modern resorts, excellent beaches and reliable sunshine throughout the year. This illustrated guide, the only readily available English language guide devoted to the island, is full of practical and background information for the holidaymaker.

The book provides advice on good restaurants, bars and nightclubs, car hire, bus routes, taxi fares and everything from tipping to purchasing time-share property.

There is a detailed section on touring routes and island excursions so that the visitor can experience the unusual beauty of the 'Island of Fire', from the fantastic geological features of the volcanic zones to the flowery valleys of the north.

£5.95   ISBN 0 900075 06 6   *Fully Illustrated*